Narrative
Pastoral Counseling

Burrell David Dinkins

Eac: May God bless you in your counseling ministry.
Burrell

xulon PRESS

Copyright © 2005 by Burrell David Dinkins

Narrative Pastoral Counseling
by Burrell David Dinkins

Printed in the United States of America

ISBN 1-597810-52-5

All rights reserved solely by the author. The author guarantees all contents are original and do not infringe upon the legal rights of any other person or work. All right reserved. No part of this book may be reproduced, stored in a retrieval system, or transmitted in any form or by any means—for example, electronic, photocopy, recording—without the prior written permission of the author. The only exception is brief quotations in printed reviews. The views expressed in this book are not necessarily those of the publisher.

Unless otherwise indicated, Bible quotations are taken from the New International Version of the Bible. Copyright © 1999 by the Holman Bible Publishers.

www.xulonpress.com

Table of Contents

✦

Chapter Six

Chapter Seven

Chapter Eight

Chapter Nine

Chapter Ten

Chapter Eleven

Chapter Twelve

This book is dedicated to my wife, Phyllis.
I'm grateful for her many years of love
and her patience to listen to my
stories

Preface

The most frequently asked question from students in my classes and workshops is: "How can I learn more about counseling from a narrative perspective?" For my seminary classes in narrative counseling I assigned required reading from several books written by other authors on narrative therapy; however no book, written from a Christian perspective, was available. They usually responded by asking: "when will you publish your book on narrative pastoral counseling?" Participants in counseling workshops in North, Central and South America ask the same question, so I decided it was time to print my ideas and stories to respond to their request.

I am grateful for the continued growth that has occurred in me because of the students I have been privileged to teach. Several of my supervisors in three years of Clinical Pastoral Education have now become friends. I'm especially grateful for my friend, Henry Close who made helpful suggestions that critiqued and encouraged me to write this book. My former colleague, Larry Losoncy, had a major influence with the chapters on grief. My therapists listened to my stories, helped me re-author many of them and encouraged me to reclaim my family story-telling tradition.

Counselees have inspired me by the originality and creativity of their stories. I was privileged to hear many of them for the first time as we created them through our counseling conversations. Some of their stories are included here. They are written in carefully disguised forms to protect their confidentiality.

Soon after arriving for a visit my granddaughter, Elizabeth will ask me to tell her a story. After listening to several newly created versions of the "Church Mouse" story she gives me a big hug and say, "Granddaddy, you are the best story teller in the world." This is when I feel blessed by all those who listened to my stories and told their stories to me.

Finally, I'm grateful to Asbury Theological Seminary with its gracious sabbatical policy. This has allowed me to spend time away from teaching and to concentrate on research and writing this manuscript.

I hope reading this book will inspire you to appreciate your own stories and give you courage to re-author those that no longer serve you well. I hope you will use what you learn from these pages to make you a more effective counselor.

Chapter One

Narrative in Pastoral Counseling

"God made man because He loves stories." Elie Wiesel

Each person is a collection of stories. Alex Haley said that the death of an old person is like a library burning down. Our personal stories are what make us human, and yours are as important as mine. Since I am writing this book I will be sharing some of my stories as well as those of others. If you want to know me you need to know my story—not a finished story, but one that I continue to create, revise, and tell myself and others who want to know me. I hope that what you read here will help you value the stories in your own life.

I grew up in a family of eleven children in the southern part of Georgia where stories were the primary means of communication. Mealtime, evenings, and weekends were my favorite times because stories were our way of learning about the world around us and the larger world beyond our own community.

Long before I learned the alphabet and the rudiments of written language, my conscious was formed by oral communication. I learned who was trustworthy, what to fear, standards of acceptable behavior, and my special place in the family. I also learned that if I wanted to tell a story, I first had to listen to the stories told by others.

My favorite people were the best storytellers. I liked going to church because special stories about people of faith were told again and again, and I even imitated our story-telling pastors right down to their mannerisms.

Unfortunately, like most children I was led to believe that school was the place where real learning took place. Without questioning this societal myth, I did what was expected by my family and required by the government—I went to school to learn how to read and write because I wanted to be as smart as my older brothers and sisters. However, school was not what I had been led to believe, and by age ten I grew bored and disinterested in book learning. I didn't know the people who wrote the books, and I found their stories unappealing because they were foreign to my everyday life.

Most of what I learned during these formative years came from listening to the stories of respected adults and later by reading the newspapers I delivered to homes before and after school. My afternoon paper route was in the segregated section of town where most of the African Americans lived. I often stopped to visit with them on their front porches and to listen to their stories.

My father had died when I was nine, and my paper route earnings were helpful to my mother. I enjoyed working but did not like going to school. This meant that I went to school out of duty and for the social contacts. I knew I could learn anything I wanted to, but I had no passion for school except in a literature class where the teacher would read the stories of great writers. She knew that I had to get up hours before sunrise to deliver newspapers and so she allowed me to sleep when I could not hold my eyes open any longer. To her surprise and the disbelief of my classmates, I received the second highest score on the final exam. In my senior year, another teacher taught the great classics of literature, using Bible stories as part of our readings. I had heard these stories in church and Sunday School, but never in the same order as in the Bible. Now they awakened in me a passion for learning that had been missing throughout public school. I felt at home with a narrative approach to learning and began to feel a call to ministry and a desire to tell the great stories of the Christian faith.

I enrolled in the college in my hometown and was accepted on academic probation, because my grade point average was so low. Finally I wanted to learn, but working full-time as a clerk in a grocery store left me little time for study. Another distraction was the availability of so many college girls to date. It was then that Mrs. Mary Love Tucker, my Sunday School teacher and favorite storyteller, realized that I was in trouble. She suggested that if I wanted to realize my vision of becoming a pastor, I think about leaving my hometown.

Without enough money for either bus fare or food for the journey, I hitchhiked the 650 miles from Valdosta, Georgia to a town in central Kentucky to attend college. I had been promised a part-time job at the college farm to pay for my room and board. Mrs. Dewberry, a personal friend of Mrs. Tucker, agreed to pay my tuition. She was a widow who had planned to send her son to college when he returned from World War II. After he was killed in action, to honor his memory she paid the tuition of other students for over forty years. I was one of her adopted sons during my college years.

In college I fell in love with learning. Simultaneously falling in love with a beautiful woman who believed in me enough to become my wife a few years later added to the joy of learning.

I yielded to the temptation of college culture to eat of the fruit of knowledge called psychology. In so doing, I rejected my storytelling culture and began thinking in the language of theory and logical analysis. Little did I know that this mythological language—in the guise of understanding and helping others with their problems— would lead me away from my true self. After college, three years of seminary taught me a lot about the facts of the Bible and theology, but little about how to listen to and tell stories. My professors regarded stories as examples or illustrations, of lesser value than logical explanations. My study of theories and techniques of counseling helped reinforce this mode of thinking and prepare me for clinical training in pastoral care and counseling. I became a loyal member of professional counseling organizations and worked thousands of hours as a pastoral counselor, marriage and family therapist, and teacher of counseling.

However, I had one major problem. Joy kept creeping into my

heart, joy that had no rational explanation. I thought it would eventually go away, but it played hide-and-seek with an occasional peek-a-boo. As any counselor trained in psychodynamics would naturally do, I tried to track the joy back to its source through reflection and personal therapy; but my search for circumstantial causes failed to produce answers. Although this joy was almost lost in my intense search for root causes, it kept coming back at the strangest times, especially when I was participating in conversations where stories were being told.

It took me a long time, but I finally realized that I would have to follow the joy. Stories are where I belong. They are my habitation, my native country, and my heritage. I live, move and have my being in them.

A joyous person lives in a world of stories, music, art, meaningful work and play. I am slowly leaving behind the land of logical analysis, though I have fond memories of lessons learned there. I hope to also leave behind a lot of baggage in that modern world as I venture into the postmodern world of narrative, with all its uncertainty. In a way, I wish it were possible to live in both worlds at the same time, but this is like wanting to travel two roads at the same time. There's a choice to be made, though sometimes I slip back into the world of modernity.

Surrounded by Stories

Stories give direction to our lives. We not only create them but also are formed and guided by them. If we wanted to run from stories, what would we be running from? How would we know they were no longer following us, demanding to be heard, even in our daydreams, or during our sleep? Death is about the only escape from stories, but even then we enter a much larger story called eternity. As John Crossan says, "We live in story as fish live in the sea." [1]

We need not look very far in our heritage to see the connection between narrative counseling and biblical narratives. These narratives are the primary means of communicating the Christian faith. Exodus, Christmas, and Easter would be impossible to understand without the stories that surround them. The organizers of the Bible canon considered the stories about Jesus too important to tell only once, and so they included four versions in the Gospels. These somewhat different versions reflect their authors, the intended readers, the time they were written, and the historical context.

In this book I give special attention to the formative effects of stories in creating our view of the world and the practicality of using a narrative approach in counseling. In this narrative approach to pastoral counseling I use Kevin Brandt's term *storying* to refer to story or narrative in pastoral conversations. *Storytelling* places the action in the one telling the story. *Storylistening* usually indicates a passive action of the one hearing the story. *Storying conversation* is a dynamic interaction between all parties in the conversation. As Brandt says, "In story both listener and teller imaginatively 'leave' the constituted self to enter an alternative story world constructed from different hypotheses, assumptions, presuppositions, and possibilities." [2]

A *narrative conversation* best portrays what I do as a pastoral counselor. Conversation is language play where both storytellers and storylisteners participate in mutually creative, interactive storying and restorying. Such conversations co-create a specific kind of knowing that is both relational and personal. This living, dynamic, constantly changing and personally present kind of knowing shapes both the knowers and the content of what is known. [3] As Brandt says, "What one receives in storying directly affects what the other can give, and what one gives directly affects what the other can receive."[4]

Narrative conversation is a unique form of communication whereby one's past experience is endowed with meaning through the storying process. Unlike a logical-scientific mode of thinking that deals with cause and effect, story conversations are imaginative creations. [5] Real events become storied events through conversation; personal experiences form the prime material with which to construct the conversation. A narrated event, as a temporal symbolization of a real event, creates space to tell and hear the larger story.

Conversation depends upon language, culture, social relationships, context, content, construction and tone of the stories. A narrated story refers to events and requires at least one author and one receiver who becomes a co-author of the interpreted events. As Mattingly and Garro claim, "Narrative allows us to not only tell what happens, but to impart how an event takes on meaning for us— to convey the 'double landscape' of inner and outer worlds." [6] Narrative conversations are powerful forms of communicating and of giving meaning to experience, especially when they are seen from a literary perspective as possessing their own plots and sub-plots.

Moving Away from the Role of Expert

I find narrative conversations to be an effective way of moving from the position of expert professional and relating more as a friend conversing on equal footing with the other parties in the conversation. As I leave behind psychological jargon, theories, and techniques, and enter into the story of another person in a support-ive co-narrating process, I discover new ways of looking at prob-lem-saturated stories and finding more hopeful solutions.

Although narrative conversation is the oldest and most funda-mental way that pastors help people, few pastors counsel from a narrative perspective. Because our formal education has been so saturated with modernity's emphasis upon linear thinking, formal logic, philosophy, and science, little attention has been paid to narrative or to conversational skills.

I see narrative conversations as landscapes painted by an artist. One scene shows the action of the characters in the painting. Other scenes portray the thoughts and feelings, or the consciousness of the characters. Jerome Bruner writes about the landscapes of action in which "the constituents are the argument of action: agent, intention or goal, situation, instrument, something corresponding to a 'story grammar.'" He defines the landscape of consciousness as "what those involved in the action know, think, or feel, or do not know, think, or feel."[7] He sees these landscapes as essential and distinct from each other. Participants in storying conversations create narratives from the landscapes of action and reflection. In a very real sense they paint the picture as they co-author the story and re-author with each other through the creation of the story during the conversation.

I regard narrative as much more than the work of gifted artists who write books, plays, and poems. It is the glue that makes life meaningful. As Barbara Hardy writes, "We dream in narrative, daydream in narrative, remember, anticipate, hope, despair, believe, doubt, plan, revise, criticize, construct, gossip, learn, hate, and love by narrative." [8]

Conversations are our most common means for making sense out of life. When I participate in a conversation, I do far more than discover information. I also participate in a way of thinking about reality. Since this happens in friend-to-friend conversations, I believe the same form of communication can be used in pastoral interchange where the primary agenda is to help people make sense of problem areas in their lives and to create a more hopeful future.

The primary difference between a friendship conversation and a narrative pastoral conversation is intentionality and flow. When I talk with a friend, I do not intend to counsel, but to share ideas and exchange stories. When I am in a helping relationship, I focus on ways to help the other person by listening more intentionally and by asking questions specifically related to the problem story that person is telling. This creates a narrative flow as we navigate together through the story.

In this book I present narrative conversation as the act and art of storying and restorying lives. Within the landscapes of action and consciousness, the conversationalists talk in the subjunctive mode as they create possibilities rather than settle for certainties.[9] This is what makes storying conversations far more than a new technique of counseling. It becomes an artistic creation with a reality all its own, when real life is understood as art.

We can see an example of a subjunctive conversation in the experience of Ann who was newly widowed. Her grief was mixed with bitterness over the death of her husband from an industrial accident until our conversations turned toward Conjectures, What if? fantasies, and desires about the future. In one conversation I asked her if she could use her imagination to create a scene where she would be a healed and happy person a year into the future. She responded with some creative scenarios of a fulfilled life. Then I asked her to consider living one day a week for the following four weeks as if this new life were real. A month later she reported feeling much better after experiencing several days of her imagined future. She thanked me for helping her make "molehills of her mountains."

Imagining Becomes Reality

Some years ago, as I pondered the ideas that eventually led to writing this book, I was faced with a personal question, "If I cannot escape stories, how can I use them in counseling?" I had not thought about their usefulness in counseling until I met Michael White from Australia and David Epston from New Zealand and became intrigued by their use of narrative in psychotherapy. Their book, *Narrative Means to Therapeutic Ends,* awoke in me an interest about how to use stories in pastoral counseling, an interest undervalued in my academic and clinical training. I felt as if I were returning to my native homeland of narrative as meaning-making.

A slow but steady shift in my thinking from a pathology-based psychology to narrative as the root metaphor or structural framework led me to use narrative in my own counseling practice. Soon afterwards I started teaching narrative pastoral counseling in classes and seminars, both in the United States and in Latin America. Each time I taught narrative pastoral conversation, some students would ask if I would write a book that would help them learn more about the subject.

Although this book has most of the basic concepts of Narrative Pastoral Counseling, it is not a systematic and detailed constructive model for NPC. Rather, I offer observations about a number of important concepts, methods and stories that should be considered.

The stories in this book are not for the purpose of illustration, demonstration, or example. Stories are far too important to be a supplement to an argument. They contain much of the meaning I want to express about narrative pastoral conversations. I have changed the names and other identifying information to protect the identity of my fellow narrative conversationalists.

Chapter Two

Storied Realities

"The stories people tell have a way of taking care of them."
Barry Lopez

O ne of my favorite books is *Crow and Weasel* by Barry Lopez. Writing from the North American Indian oral tradition, he tells the story of two young braves who dare to venture further north than anyone in their tribe had ever gone. They leave early one spring day and make their perilous journey until they come to the Inuit people. Their hosts treat them as honored guests, not only by caring for their physical needs but also by listening to their stories, and telling them stories of their own people.

As summer ends the two braves start their long trip home. They are slowed down and their lives endangered by an earlier winter than anticipated. As they journey on horseback, they meet Badger who extends hospitality by inviting them to spend the night in her den. She offers them food and shelter, but then does something more significant by inviting them to tell their stories. After they have eaten, she asks, "Now tell me, my friends, what did you see up north? I have always wanted to know what it is like there."

Badger does more than listen passively. She helps Weasel and Crow tell their stories by asking questions that encourage them to give detailed descriptions of their journey. Toward the end of the storytelling, Crow says, "We are grateful for your hospitality, Badger. Each place we go we learn something, and your wisdom here has helped us." Although Badger is the listening host and talks little, yet Crow thanks her for her wisdom. Finally, Badger makes a suggestion:

> "I would ask you to remember only this one thing, The stories people tell have a way of taking care of them. If stories come to you, care for them. And learn to give them away where they are needed. Sometimes a person needs a story more than food to stay alive. That is why we put stories in each other's memory. This is how people care for themselves." [10]

One of the best ways to care for people is to care for their stories. This is why we should treat our conversations as opportunities for hospitality. In his Rule for the Benedictine Order that Saint Benedict founded he wrote that the stranger visiting the monastery was to be treated with hospitality as if that person were Jesus Christ. Such respect for others includes a special interest in their stories, in somewhat the same way that Mary treated Jesus during His visit with her and her sister Martha in their home in Bethany. People who learn to listen with love also learn to listen to their own stories and discover the gift of listening to God.

Someone who wants to talk about a personal problem usually tells a story about the problem. Something in that person's experience has turned from being life-producing to being problematic. The first step in helping is to listen to both the thoughts and the feelings. The next step is to pay special attention to the person's stories, just as if they were artistically created especially for this conversation. Although interpretations and actions also are integrated into the narrative, the complete story is more important than any one element of it.

Most stories are about trouble—someone did a wrong or had an accident. Yet, stories also offer solutions to the problems. The trouble is quite easily identified, but solutions often hide within the problem stories until someone goes looking for them. The role of the narrative counselor is to assist in developing the solution story. Listening to the problem story is not enough. What counselees need from a counselor is not answers for their problems but a better story that will give them hope. New stories created by the person with the problem give the most hope, because the creator owns the story. The primary role of the helper is to assist in the development of a more hopeful and future-oriented story.

Through several counseling sessions Carol struggled through painful memories of her abusive extended family, yet discovered that in the midst of this she had created important values that guided her life to a more meaningful existence. She used her last counseling sessions to create a vision for the future through storying what it would look like at different seasons of her life. For her last session she requested that I serve communion to her. Her last words were: "thank you for changing the story of my life."

Carl Rogers exerted a major influence on my early training in counseling. Through his books and in my clinical training under experienced supervisors, I learned how to listen with empathy to other people. I discovered that what hurting people want most is not answers to their problems, but someone who cares and is patient enough to really listen to them. Rogers wrote:

A number of times in my life I have felt myself bursting with insoluble problems, or going round and round in tormented circles or, during one period, overcome by feelings of worthlessness and despair... I have been able to find individuals who have been able to hear me and thus rescue me from the chaos of my feelings and who have been able to hear my meanings a little more deeply than I have known them...can testify that when you are in psychological stress and someone hears you without passing judgment on you, without trying to take responsibility for you, without trying to mold you...has permitted me to bring out the frightening feelings, the guilt, the despair, the confusions...It is astonishing how elements that seem insoluble become soluble when someone listens, how confusions which seemed irremediable turn relatively clear flow-streams when one is heard. [11]

Carl Rogers helped me integrate the affective life of counseling with my earlier focus on thoughts and behaviors. From him and from my supervisors, I learned to appreciate the importance of listening for feelings in a counseling relationship. A narrative approach to conversations uses empathic listening skills—especially in the early phase of the conversation, but moves beyond thoughts, feelings and behaviors to an intense interest in the stories counselees tell.

When people trapped by physical and mental limitations find a person who listens, really listens, to their stories so that they know they have been heard, they do not feel as alone as before. I can listen for meanings better when I am not trying to fit what I hear into a particular theoretical framework, for I can really pay attention to the story itself.

I listen with what I call "an unknowing attitude." This does not mean that I know nothing at all or have no opinions of my own. My mind is not in neutral when I listen. Rather, I take a position of curiosity somewhat like a newspaper reporter, seeking as much of the story as possible in order to recreate as faithfully as possible the essence of the story. It is not that I am looking for something hidden that is waiting to come out, for I believe that stories create meaning in the very act of telling and listening. Through the telling of the story the storyteller comes to understand that which could not be understood without the conversation. The conversation itself creates a new perspective, a new meaning. Unexpected things begin to happen as new understandings are created.

Mutual storying conversations are opportunities for learning together rather than discovering some truth that is waiting to appear. As the pain from the problem story is relived and heard with respect, a new story is created. The narrative conversationalist carefully takes apart the old story and helps reconstruct a new one with the storyteller. Narrative listening, as well as narrative telling, creates new versions of the story and this, in turn, creates new meanings. These new meanings, and the actions that flow from them, are the essence of the art of storying conversations.

I try to remember that someone telling stories to me always depends upon my ability to listen and to express interest in the story. A personal story about a problem will be told to me differently than it will be told to another person. Men tell stories to other men differently than they tell them to women. Stories are modified to fit into another person's frame of reference and social context.

Active Listening

From observing those I consider to be good listeners, I notice that they often interrupt. They are involved in a dynamic interchange of the shifting turns of speaker and listener. Each party in the conversation invests energy in the dialogue. The major difference is that the primary listener in the conversation cares enough to stay attentive to the story of the primary speaker. Questions are asked to clarify, expand and focus the story without making an effort to shift the conversation to another subject.

Active listening is an important skill for a pastor, but it is not enough. When a person is grieving, the listening takes on a different quality and tone. The empathic listener makes few comments, but those he or she does make are well chosen. A good listener may ask a few questions to facilitate the telling of the story about the deceased, but the main concern is to offer a conversational relationship that facilitates expression of the grief and offers emotional support.

When I am engaged in narrative counseling, I try to speak as naturally as possible, using everyday words. I seek to avoid judging, diagnosing, explaining, telling people what to do about their problems, or taking on the air of a professional counselor. I believe in caring for people by conversing with them so that they can discover how their stories will help or hinder them. A conversational approach is less stressful and more interesting than a problem-oriented approach to counseling. Instead of ending a counseling day drained of energy, I find that I am energized and inspired by the stories counselees and I create together.

Inside—Outside Conversations

Focusing on the stories of people, rather than listening to their problems in order to make a diagnosis or to find the root cause of a problem, underscores the difference between the inductive and deductive approaches to pastoral conversations. Knowledge usually flows from the particular out to broader understandings. An *inductive* approach to knowing through stories moves from the smaller to the larger message. The bits and pieces of the story are expanded through a "not knowing" (acknowledging that I do not know) attitude on the part of the counselor who will ask sincere questions to get a broader perspective of the story.

A *deductive* approach to pastoral conversations goes the other direction, the listener focusing on the story to find bits and pieces of information that fit into a specific way of thinking. Unfortunately, this approach shifts ownership of the story from the teller to the listener who then claims the power to name and define the meaning of the story. The teller loses agency or power over the story. I do not believe this is the best way to be with the people in pastoral conversations. They are more effectively helped when they maintain ownership of their own stories and, in turn, of their lives, as they are being revised during the sharing of the stories. This helps them develop both the freedom and the responsibility for the new meanings, strength, and actions they find through the pastoral conversations.

Of course, some deductive conversations are appropriate. I expect my mechanic and my physician to listen to what I say, whether in stories or direct explanations, in order to use deductive logic, make a good diagnosis, and suggest effective remedies for the problem. But, I do not want my pastor to listen to me this way.

Listening with Large Ears

A good conversation is more effective when the helper "listens with large ears." This metaphor for listening comes from Elochukwu E. Uzukwu, an African Christian leader who has special interest in the ministry gifts that serve the Christian community. [12] According to Uzukwu, the totem for the leader among the Manja people of Central Africa is the rabbit because this small and non-threatening animal has large ears. The leader of the tribe is like the rabbit, because listening with large ears brings the leader close to the conversations of the people, to God, and to the ancestors. The leader is the custodian of the word and the stories of the community.

The function of the leader is to receive the word through listening in conversation. When the sacred word, Scripture, is spoken to listening ears, it heals and provides direction for the community. The sacred word is much too large for the mouth. It belongs to the narrative life of the whole community. It is a part of the *palaver* (spoken word) of the community that is liberated through the ministry "with large ears" that cares for the word by caring for the stories of the people and the stories of the people of God in Scripture.

In suggesting that we listen with large ears, I mean that we help people as we facilitate the telling of their stories. When they tell their stories they both receive and give help in a communal context. Both the telling of stories and listening to stories form a reciprocal dynamic of community building. If there are no stories, there is no community. If there is no community, there are fewer and fewer healthy stories. When the stories stop, the community dies.

I like the communal model of care and counseling in Africa and Latin America, because it involves intense listening to the Spirit and to the narrative life of one another in community. Uzukwu believes that if the voices of the people are not listened to, arrogance and power will dominate the life of the leader and the life of the church. If people listen only to the stories of their leader, but the leader does not listen to them, the stories of the people will be stifled and impoverished. This in turn will diminish the life of the community.

Many pastors find it extremely difficult to really listen to the people's stories, even in counseling sessions. They need to remember that listening itself is a ministry, not merely a prelude to helping. Dietrich Bonhoeffer wrote about listening in the Christian community:

The first service that one owes to others in the fellowship consists in listening to them. Just as love to God begins with listening to His Word, so the beginning of love for the brethren is learning to listen to them. It is God's love for us that He not only gives us His Word but also lends us His ear. So it is His work that we do for our brothers and sisters when we learn to listen to them. Christians. . .so often think that they must always contribute something when they are in the company of others, that this is the one service they have to render. They forget that listening can be a greater service than speaking.[13]

Conversational Hospitality

When I invite people to my home, I treat them with the courtesies of hospitality. I take responsibility for their comfort and well-being to help them feel safe and glad to be my guests. I welcome them as they are. Listening to their stories is the most important part of being a good host. In a similar way, when I enter into a pastoral conversation with someone, I am the host of the flow of the conversation between us. If my concern and care is genuine, they will reveal their inner world to me as I invite them to share conversation. No matter where the conversation takes place, in a home, while sharing a meal together, during a hospital visit, conversing after a church meeting, talking by phone or visiting in my office, I can still host the conversation.

One of the best stories I heard about hosting a conversation comes from Bill, a former student. He told the Narrative Pastoral Counseling class about going out to dinner on Valentine's Day with his wife, Sally. After ordering their meal, Bill noticed an elderly man seated by himself. Though he was a total stranger, there was something about him that caused Bill to feel empathy for him. He told Sally that he wished he could talk with this man. When she suggested that he take advantage of this opportunity, he responded, "I know we came here to have a special dinner together, and yet, I'd like to ask him if we could eat with him." They discussed what it could mean to share their meal with a stranger on Valentine's Day. Sally said she would be willing to eat with the man, if that was what Bill felt led to do.

They went to his table and politely asked if they could eat their meal with him. He acted both surprised and overjoyed, as if relieved not to have to eat alone. After they introduced themselves, the old man talked about his wife and their forty years of marriage. With tears running down his cheeks, he told them about her death only a few months earlier. He shared with them how much he dreaded Valentine's Day because they had always had a dinner date on that day. They asked him to tell them more about his wife. As they shared dinner with this man, they listened with great interest to his stories about many years of a happy marriage. Bill and Sally told him they had been married only two years and would like to hear about how he and his wife had built such a good marriage.

As Bill and Sally co-hosted the stories of this fortunate stranger, he shared many helpful ideas that Bill and Sally wanted to include in their marriage. This happened because they honored his memories, his stories, and his tears. When they left the restaurant, they felt even greater love for each other for having listened to the love story of the stranger and his wife. They had cared for him by caring for his stories. They did not try to help by fixing his grief, but by loving him through hosting his stories. The stories expressed his personhood. No longer was he a stranger to them, for his stories were the connecting link to their own love story.

Chapter Three

Narrative Conversations

"A genuine conversation gives me access to thoughts
that I did not know myself capable of, that I was not capable of."
Maurice Marleau-Ponty

Making the shift to using the word *conversation* instead of *counseling* has not been easy for me. Sometimes I find myself using both words to refer to the same thing. In most of my ministry, I used *counseling* or *therapy* when referring to the pastor's role in helping people with personal and family problems. Most of the literature is listed under these terms. I made the change after reflecting on how much of the total communication by pastors is done through conversation, mainly in story form.

I had also begun paying more attention to my contact with people during the week. At first glance this had not appeared significant, just taken for granted. My initial response was, "Of course, we communicate more through conversation than any other way. Everyone does, so why focus on it? Why spend time on a natural way of talking when other kinds of communication in ministry need more attention?" Yet, as I paid attention to my own way of conversing and listening to counselees, the more interested I became.

My interest never took me toward logical or technical analysis of the content of the conversations. Nor am I primarily concerned in the interpersonal and intrapersonal dynamics of conversations, though these are certainly important.

What I wanted to find was a more wholistic way of being with people, one that included verbal exchanges but went beyond this to the quality of being in relationship with others. The modern counseling movement has its origins in rationalism with strong emphasis on the counselor being an objective observer with expert knowledge and skills. Believing that this approach is too limited to express the totality of a pastoral helping relationship, I wanted to recapture the richness of the word *conversation.*

Religious Conversation

John Wesley used the word *conversation* in his letters, sermons, and ciphered diary. In his diary he included the initials *RC* to mean "religious conversation."

> We have had our conversation: the Apostle in the original expresses this by one single word *anestraphemen* but the meaning thereof is exceedingly broad, taking in our whole department, yea, every inward as well as outward circumstance, whether relating to our soul or body. It includes every motion of the heart, of our tongue, of our hands, and bodily members. It extends to all our actions and words; to the employment of all our powers and faculties, to the manner of using every talent we have received, with respect either to God or Man. [14]

Wesley knew nothing about modern counseling concepts, but he did understand the importance of conversation as a way of being with another. He believed that a person's conversation included what we would call character, behavior, reputation, and personal attributes. When I use the term *pastoral conversation* as synonymous for pastoral counseling, I am emphasizing the natural flow of communication in a conversational relationship of respect and mutuality. I see such conversational dialogue as a means of bringing people together in a relationship of sharing with ethical boundaries.

Specialists and Generalists

Specialists occupy a distinct place in counseling and psychotherapy; however, these are not the people who do most of the helping ministry in the church. When specialists are available and affordable, and when their religious value system is compatible with a given church, they can serve as valuable referral resources. Unfortunately, the overemphasis on the specialist, now more closely identified with the medical establishment than with the church, creates the impression that pastors are incapable of helping people because they lack expertise in pathology-based language and techniques of treating medical conditions.

My concern is that specialists not create a sense of incompetence in pastors. A pastor's expertise flows from communication with people through telling and listening to stories. Most pastors have a special facility for listening and talking with people. We do not need the old model of pastor as someone with expert knowledge who considers counselees as consumers of this knowledge. This is what one writer has called "the expert and the dummy model."

The medical model for counseling is only one way to do pastoral effectiveness. Medical diagnosticians listen to stories in order to gather information about a problem, formulate a diagnosis, and apply a specific modality of treatment. Categorizing people with diagnostic labels can easily become a means of domination over others and therefore inappropriate in pastoral relationships. Too frequently this leads to attributing guilt or blame, thus further complicating the problem. [15]

By shifting from a concern for finding the cause and location of a problem to a focus on the stories that surround the problem, pastors can increase their effectiveness in helping people. Letting go of the need to have expert knowledge of causes, effects and answers to solve people's problems can create new sense of freedom and joy in counseling.

Pastoral effectiveness depends upon how well we facilitate the mutual exploration of the stories people share with us. In my conversations I try to develop with the other party more hopeful stories as the conversation progresses. Rather than thinking that my knowledge of the problem can provide the solution, I focus on helping the counselee explore possibilities and learn from our conversation.

In the act of conversing, their old stories are reauthored into mutually created stories. Because each party has a special way of viewing the stories, we both contribute to rewriting them. Neither party is superior to the other, for each respects the viewpoint of the other and learns from the conversation. The dialogical conversation itself provides the help, not some previously hidden knowledge brought to awareness. This does not negate the fact that each party brings a considerable background of information to the conversation that contributes to the flow of the dialogue.

I do not mean to suggest that all pastoral conversation is counseling. Rather, I am using *conversation* as a metaphor to move away from the notion that counseling is mainly advice or therapy. People are not objects to be changed by telling them to do specific things; they are not sick persons to be healed. They are individuals looking for a more hopeful story. While giving advice is easy, it also creates a temptation to abuse the power of a pastoral relationship.

Co-Creating Stories

I see such narrative conversations as artistic creations. The more I pay special attention to how all parties in the conversation function as both actors and joint authors of the stories told in the conversations, the more artistic they appear to me. Like any art, they require constant practice and reflection. Pastors who have a natural talent for storytelling can also develop the art of listening and appropriately responding to stories in pastoral conversations.

I see myself as a co-producer of the counselee's stories, primarily through the questions I ask. My primary interest now is to learn more about the role of questions in pastoral conversations, in order to facilitate the authoring and reauthoring of stories. I do this by paying attention to the way I converse in helping conversations. At first this concentration felt awkward, but over time I was able to meta-communicate about my conversations. By this I mean to communicate with myself about the way I was interacting during a conversation. Like any new skill, this needed a lot of discipline at first, and I found it very tiring. Yet, even occasionally monitoring how I was communicating helped me develop a more reflective attitude in my conversations.

Narrative conversations require personal discipline to keep control over memories of past experiences similar to the stories I am hearing at the moment. My mind naturally finds connections between the present story and some previous experience in my own life or stories I have filed away in memory. My personal memories serve me best when I do not break into another person's story to share my own.

I feel a great deal of excitement as I approach each person as a mystery story waiting to be told. I can best hear the story when I am willing to be curious and take an unknowing approach, rather than to listen for bits and pieces of information that may fit into a predetermined frame of reference. When I listen creatively, new and often very different stories emerge, and may be unlike what the person telling the stories intended them to be. There is no script, only the co-authoring of a new story from the elements of previous experiences.

In narrative pastoral conversations, stories are seen as the primary means of helping people, rather than as illustrations to help make a point. Neither should they be seen merely as a source of information. Indeed, they do contain a lot of information, but that is not the purpose of the conversation.

The primary task of a pastoral conversationalist is to develop a relationship that promotes dialogue. Help comes through the narrative interchange. The stories people choose to tell, and the way they choose to tell them, depends upon the quality of the relationship and the purpose of the conversation. I try to keep in mind the following questions: "Why is this person telling me this story? Why is it being told now? How is it being told to me?" Telling and listening create new meanings and new alternatives. As a participant in a pastoral conversation, my role is to help create a dialogical relationship in which the speakers and listeners can present themselves as persons. [16]

When people come to me for help, they tell stories about concerns that precipitated the conversation in the first place. We have to decide which story or segment of a story we will give attention to as we hold up our conversational mirror. A story is not told the same way twice, no matter how many times it may be repeated. With each telling it is recreated, revised and re-framed. Often parts of the story not previously perceived as important become a key part of the restorying.

My role is to help people find new alternative stories that enable them to take action against the problems they face. Both telling and listening alter the stories and their meanings. Questions and comments, or the lack thereof, influence the creation of the stories. Other parts of the story and substories remain unattended. While telling a story about a significant experience, a story teller may say to me, "Wow, I never thought of that before!"

I have noticed that the people who have helped me the most over the years were very present during the conversations, paying close attention to my story. They took me, and my story seriously and became a participant in helping me discover new meanings as we talked. This would not have happened without the conversation.

Usually it is best to wait until the other party comes to a stopping place before asking a question or returning to the part of the story that I choose to comment on or ask for more detail. Sometimes I do this by asking, "You said . . . I wonder if you could tell me more about that." I may ask a present, past, or future-oriented question. In the early stage of the conversation, I usually talk more about the present and some about the past. As the conversation develops, I ask more future-oriented questions.

The beginnings and endings of pastoral conversations are especially important; the purpose of the conversation needs to be clearly established early on, and the person seeking help needs to know the conversation was worthwhile by the way it ends. As we begin, I ask myself, "What does this person need to get out of this conversation?" The answer may not be evident at first. Before we finish I ask myself, "Did this person get what he or she came to talk with me about, or what needs to be talked about?"

A "Not-Knowing" Mind-set

The formal education of pastors can unintentionally lead them to believe that they should have the solutions for problems, or know how to find the answers. This comes from taking exams, writing research papers and responding to didactic questions asked in class.

I suggest that pastoral conversationalists work from a strong sense of curiosity along with a "not- knowing" mind-set. Not-knowing means putting aside prior explanations, and pre-understandings and interpretations based upon personal experiences, knowledge, or theoretical formulas.[17] Instead of an expert, all-knowing counselor, there is an all-inquiring conversationalist with an impish curiosity to discover.

Good conversations are more than the discovery of some truth about life or finding the answer to a difficult problem. Instead, they aid in developing a new, mutually created story that is more satisfying than the older one. When conversationalists respect each other, they reach outside of the personal internal dialogue to discover new perspectives on the story, thereby revising it and creating a new one. Satisfying conversations are more like teamwork on a project in which each party has a vested interest in the outcome. They become co-creators of a new story. Though each party has a different perspective they have enough in common to keep the conversation flowing until a new narrative emerges to replace the older one. The focus is on the creation of a more edifying story than on a search for some objective truth about the situation. The effectiveness of the conversation depends upon the creation of a more redemptive story that provides a vision for a hopeful future.

I think about narrative pastoral conversations as a complementary relationship based upon equality, one soul conversing with another soul. Each one brings a special contribution to the conversation. They participate as co-authors in the creation of the stories told in the conversation and each one is affected by these stories. Conversation is the medium for counseling, and stories are the content. The Holy Spirit is the third participant in the conversation.

Each person I talk with is an expert on his or her own life. People tell me what they want me to know by telling stories about their lives. I do not look at stories as illustration, or primarily information about the problem. Stories that once were seen as finished narratives can be revised to be more hopeful and useful to solve specific personal problems. [18]

Though listening to the story is basic, I do far more than just listen. I also help construct the story and, when the conversation is effective, help to reconstruct a life. We become co-artists creating something that could not have existed without our dialogical conversation.

Stories do not just happen to people. They are created and have a powerful effect upon their creator and to a lesser degree upon the co-creator listener. In order to make sense of life, people have to create meaningful narratives about specific events. The events are important, but the stories about them are even more important.

Modernity to Postmodernity

The period from the Renaissance to the 1970's has been called the "Age of Modernity." Attention was focused on giving meaning to events through explaining, interpreting, and arguing for rational understandings. In our Postmodern Age, narrative pastoral conversations are more suitable because they focus on the stories rather than on an analysis of the information contained in them. No one tells a complete story because no story can capture the richness of an experience. The portions left out, especially the exceptions to the theme of the story, may be as important as the parts included in the story. Stories are present experiences as much as described past experiences. They create reality from what has been experienced and, in turn, create new experiences from the telling.

Most books on the pastoral counseling relationship focus on the verbal expressions and hidden thoughts and feelings of the counselees. Conversations are analyzed to propose an objective evaluation of the information gained from the exchanges between the counselor and the counselee. Stories are considered a means for gaining information, not as an art form of counseling ministry as I am suggesting.

In one of the few books on the conversational approach to

counseling, *The Art of Pastoral Conversation* by Heije Faber and Ebel van der Schoot, the authors were concerned about conversations as a source of information about the psychodynamics of the counselee, rather than the story-creation process as counseling. They wrote, "How can we converse hopefully with our people? How can we analyze what it is we are doing in conversation, not only in our pastoral counseling but also in the many kinds of contacts, relatively formal or otherwise, that we have? How can we be ourselves, and still be responsible in our conversations?" [19]

They approached pastoral conversation with the paradigm of psychoanalysis, looking for hidden meanings in the stories told during conversations so they could discover the essence of the problem. They found what they looked for, as they listened to stories with an ear for the thoughts and the feelings of the counselees in order to gain a rational understanding of the counselees. They gave no attention to the structure of the stories and the kinds of questions asked during counseling. Questions were kept at a minimum to keep from indicating too much interest in information. Instead they waited for opportune moments to facilitate cathartic expression of feelings—their goal for the pastoral counseling.

Writing in the context of the 1960s, they used conversation to discover what was going on inside the counselee. This modern approach to pastoral counseling was based upon Naturalism, with its tendency towards a causal explanation of thoughts, feeling and behavior, modeled after psychoanalysis. This marked a shift in the focus of pastoral counselors. No longer would pastoral counseling be understood as just a rational exchange of words in a conversation. The exploration into the domain of feelings became the primary concern. "In pastoral conversations it is not just the words spoken but rather the feelings which both partners possess and show (or perhaps hide) that determine the development of the conversation and that the one who is leading the conversation—here the minister—must be expected to pay attention to this." [20]

Douglas Purnell's book: *Conversation as Ministry* uses the sharing of stories in pastoral conversations to help people tell of their experiences of living. He sees story-sharing as the primary means of pastoral care. He says, "When you walk with people into the spaces of silence and/or chaos, you are walking into the space into which the voice of God breaks in fresh ways." [21]

Building upon this modern approach to pastoral conversations, I propose a postmodern idea to the narrative potential of pastoral conversations where reality and meaning are created through dialogical storied conversation and action. Knowledge of experience and events is a relational process generated by language in a social context through the exchange of stories. This leads me to the conviction that the next revolution in the caring ministry of the church will happen when we realize that "meaning creation" through storytelling and storylistening represents the mind and spirit equivalent of the body's immune system.

The Spirituality of Conversation

I see pastoral conversations as a spiritual relationship. Troubled persons have stories to tell and they want to be heard, understood, responded to. In turn, they want to respond to our reactions. They need a depth of understanding from their pastor, a depth that depends upon the presence of the Holy Spirit as the third party in the conversation. This assumes that the words of Jesus are trustworthy: "Where two or three come together in my name, there I am with them" (Matthew 18:20, NIV.). Belief in the presence of the Holy Spirit in pastoral conversations greatly relieves counselors and can prevent them from over-functioning. They can expect healing to take place without anxiously pushing to make it happen. They can also invite mystery, and expect unknowing creative imagination and the process of dialogue to be stimulated and aided by the invisible but dynamic work of the Spirit.

After Ann and I had conversed for a time, we had several minutes of silence in our conversation. Then she said to me, "This room is like a sanctuary for me. With you I can be real because I also feel that I am in the presence of God. The death of my husband a year ago was a considerable loss to me; but now, to also accept my relief from the verbal abuse is a blessing. I realize now that I loved him, but I am also aware that I hated him at times. Your acceptance of my anger and hatred helps me accept myself. I believe I can accept God's forgiveness for me. This is helping me release my husband to a merciful God." Her confession came after our restorying conversations about her marriage. It would not have been possible without the presence of the Third Party in the narrative conversation.

In a sense all conversations are narrative and carry a healing potential. However, narrative pastoral conversations are for the purpose of alleviating suffering in persons with problems and to facilitate the healing power of God through stories created during the conversation in the presence of the Holy Spirit. The pastor, or a gifted and trained lay-person, enters the conversation without a specific agenda for the conversation but as a way of being the incarnational presence of Christ for others. All persons in the conversation are participant storytellers, though the focus of the story creation is primarily on the person being helped.

Genuine narrative pastoral conversations open the way for thoughts and feelings wrapped in stories that the parties in the conversation could not have previously known. The role of the narrative pastoral counselor is to create an environment in which people can tell their stories, feel their pain and their joy, and then discover their competencies and their faith in God who is the author and finisher of all our stories.

Chapter Four

Storying Solutions Instead
of Problem-Solving

"Sooner or later, I have to give up my hope of a better past."

Walter was four months old when my wife and I took him to
Brazil. His five-year-old brother and two-year-old sister
soon made the shift from English to the Portuguese language of
their Brazilian playmates. A year later they were speaking Portuguese better than my wife and I, even though we had completed a
year of language school. When Walter started talking he chose the
language of his Brazilian friends. He understood English, since we
spoke it in our home, but he and his siblings responded to us in
Portuguese. When my wife home-schooled him with English
kindergarten materials, he understood the English but resisted
speaking it. After we moved to city of Apucarana in the state of
Parana he played with his Japanese playmates in their language and
with his Polish playmates in their language, as well as speaking
Portuguese with his Brazilian friends.

Our family returned to the United States a few months before
Walter entered the first grade and soon he was speaking English and
refusing to speak in Portuguese. Three months into first grade his

teacher called to tell us that Walter was not learning how to read in English like his classmates. After talking with the teacher about his years in Brazil, I suggested that she give him time to feel more comfortable with the use of the English language. I assured her that he would catch up with the other students, but asked her to call again if he didn't make enough progress. I also talked with Walter about his reading and encouraged him to do his best in school.

Two months later the teacher called again. With frustration in her voice she told how concerned she was about Walter. She asked permission to have him tested by the school psychologist because she was convinced that he had a learning disability. I became very concerned and started feeling guilty for subjecting him to such culturally diverse living conditions. The waiting time was over; we had to take some action. However, I did not want to give permission for testing until I had another chance to talk with Walter about school.

After sharing my concerns with my wife, I accepted the responsibility for having a serious conversation with him. I waited until she was at a church choir practice to get Walter alone for a private conversation in the master bedroom. Soon we were bouncing gleefully on the bed. We knew this was a prohibited activity, but the one who prohibited it was at choir practice. Several minutes of bouncing and playing left us exhausted as we collapsed on the bed to rest. I decided this was the time to ask Walter about his reading.

I chose a not-knowing-but-wanting-to-learn approach by posing a question, "Walter, I'm puzzled. I don't understand why you're not learning to read."

After a few moments of silence, Walter responded, "I am not reading because I don't want to learn how to read in English and I'm not going to learn."

Surprised by his answer, I asked, "Why not? Your parents like reading and your brother and your sister like to read. Why don't you want to learn how to read?

The response came immediately, "Daddy, have you ever stopped to think, if I learn how to read just one of those books, how many I will have to read?"

Recovering from shock at such a simple but profound response from a six-year-old's understanding of his present and future reality,

I tried to challenge his perception. "If you learn how to read, then you can read any book you want." I knew this was not an accurate statement, because he would spend many years reading books required by his teachers. I was still trying to digest the secret of his personal story about not learning to read. Instead of pushing the issue into a power struggle, I decided it would be wise to stop our conversation and ask Walter to help remake the bed before his mother got home.

My wife and I stayed up late that night discussing this surprising part of Walter's story. We decided the next step would be to call the teacher to let her in on the secret. After relating the story of my conversation with Walter, I asked the teacher to show some interest in class to Walter's cross-cultural background and language abilities in Portuguese, to see if this would help him want to learn how to read in English. Reluctantly she agreed, but still insisted that he had a learning disability. She firmly warned that if he failed first grade it was not going to be her responsibility. She did not believe it was a "want to" disability created by the way he authored his own life story.

The next evening at the dinner table, I asked Walter what had happened at school that day. His response was:

"Oh, not much."

Curious, I probed further.

"Did the teacher ask you to do anything different?"

"Well, she did ask me to teach the class to say something in Portuguese."

When he said no more, I could stand only so much not-knowing and so I asked,

"What did you teach the class?"

"Oh, I taught them to say thank you."

"What did you tell them to say?"

"I told them to say, 'Aregato.'"

Anxious to correct his mistake, I said,

"That's not Portuguese. That's the Japanese word for thank you."

Walter shot back,

"O Dad, I know that, but those kids don't know it. They think they are so smart because they can read in English. They don't even know the difference between Portuguese and Japanese."

When our family finally stopped laughing, I told him, with the straightest face I could put on, that he should prove that he could learn to read English words. Walter accepted the challenge and soon caught up with the rest of his classmates.

Walter had his own unique story about language. His story included the hope of our family moving back to Brazil where he could speak and read in the language most comfortable to him. The teacher's story was created from her training in learning disabilities that did not include unique language skills from another culture. The diagnostic categories failed her in Walter's case—she was so focused on his problem that she did not try to discover the story behind the problem or any possible exceptions to the problem as she saw it. Her focus on his reading problem caused that problem to gain power.

Problem Orientation vs. Solution Orientation

A big difference exists between a problem-centered approach in pastoral conversations and a solution-oriented approach. Problem-oriented conversations focus primarily on what is wrong, what isn't working. Something wrong happened and blame is usually targeted toward the person perceived to be the cause of the wrong. Naturally, this causes defensiveness on the part of the person being blamed. No one likes to be put in this position—no individual and no group. The story of a young pastor, told in a letter, illustrates the difference between these approaches. I'll let Pastor Tom tell his story.

"When I was appointed to my first church, I soon began to feel that something there was not right. Everyone seemed friendly, but distant. I wondered what were they keeping from me. They seemed to be hesitant to speak about the history of the church. I wondered what direction we should go if I did not know where we were.

My analyzer went to work. I like to look at situations and figure them out. Diagnosis was my game. I thought,

'Surely there must be some causes that can be found, analyzed and fixed. If I find the problem, I can find the answer.' I thought I had pinpointed some of the problems and suggested ways to fix them, but no one wanted to do anything about them. Everyone continued to be quiet. This was about to drive me crazy because I did not know how to fix their problems.

After eight months, the church leaders asked me to leave at the end of a year. Instead of becoming bitter, I decided to preach the best I could and love them as they were. In three months another meeting was held and they voted for me to stay. I remembered how I had gone into the church like a mechanic wanting to fix things. Then I discovered that my job was to love the people, preach the Word, and allow God to do the work. God was working to help me understand what it meant to have a not-knowing attitude, but to let Him be the all-knowing One.

I learned a lot in that first church. God helped me change from mechanic to pastor. The more I listened to their stories through dialogical conversations with them, the more I liked them. As I demonstrated interest in them, they expressed more interest in my ideas, in my stories."

Shifting the Focus

Unfortunately, our thoughts and conversations so easily turn toward problems. I am not suggesting that pastoral counselors should take a Pollyanna approach. What I am suggesting is that the primary conversational motive be toward creating solutions, rather than remaining in the vortex of the problem.

I used to think that the more I helped people talk about their problems, the better they would feel and act. This belief was the result of my education and training in counseling in which I was taught to peel back the layers of awareness about problems until we reached the core issues, mostly unconscious ones. I know that I did help many people, but I realize now that we wasted time and energy through our problem-focused conversations. Just sharing the thoughts and feelings related to problems did not resolve them, even though sometimes people felt better after sharing their problem-saturated stories in a caring counseling relationship.

There are appropriate times and places for talking about problems. However, I don't want a diagnosis from my pastor, nor do I want him to fix me. I want my pastor to listen to me as I tell my story and then help me find meaning and hope. When I talk about a specific problem, I may need help in discovering what I need to change in my life, but I don't need to be diagnosed or typed. Neither do I need sympathy. I find it much easier to face difficulties when I am seen as competent in most areas of my life. Sometimes I may even need to be reminded of this when I focus only on my problems, when I am not affirming my abilities and tend to doubt myself. I want to know that my pastor believes in my ability to resolve life issues. The best way to demonstrate this is by asking sensitive and creative questions as we talk together. The quality of these questions shows whether my pastor has confidence in my ability to solve my own problems.

Where Is the Problem?

"The person is not the problem; the problem is the problem." [22] This sentence expresses one of the most important insights that I've come across in my ministry, because it has such profound implications for working with people. I've discovered a lot of freedom in this simple statement—the freedom to stop focusing on persons as problems.

Neither do I think that the problem is in the relationship between persons. Rather, the person's relationship to the problem becomes my focus. I no longer spend much time with the history of a problem because I now believe there is little connection between how a problem was created and how it is resolved. Rather, I concentrate on the story as a narrative with a life of its own. Also, I look for exceptions to the problem dynamics—areas of life where the counselee is succeeding at something and has a sense of accomplishment. Then together we seek ways to apply knowledge or techniques from these areas of success to the problem. We look for some small changes that will likely bring satisfactory results and, in turn, alter the story of the problem. These small changes have a way of initiating even greater changes.

I have also become much more future-focused in my conversations. I find this to be more productive than spending most of the time talking about the problems of the past. The difference between the two approaches reminds me of driving a car. It is wiser to spend most of my driving time looking ahead through the windshield and much less time looking at what lies behind in the rearview mirror. Driving an automobile without a rearview mirror can be unsettling and dangerous. But, it is even more dangerous to drive with a fogged windshield. Counseling conversations should place more importance on creating stories about the future, yet without neglecting the stories of the past. The past is best understood from the perspective of the future.

I've observed how couples caught in a struggle to discover the "truth" of what happened in their relationship tend to argue a lot over each other's interpretation of the truth. They become more interested in winning an argument than in resolving their problems. I do my best to stay out of this trap. I've discovered the hard way that asking questions that focus too much on problems often causes the conversation to go in circles. Also, the problems themselves may gain power over the conversation. I now try to remember how much easier it is to make problems worse than it is to make them better. Unfortunately, most serious problems are created by someone's attempts to resolve problems.

I look for signs of hope and an accompanying enthusiasm and energy for life. This approach to counseling energizes all parties in the conversation. My fatigue level decreased considerably when I shifted from a problem focus to a solution orientation.

Chapter Five

Asking Good Questions

"It is better to ask some of the questions than to know
all the answers"

James Thurber

I have already suggested that asking thoughtful and timely questions is the key to narrative conversations. In this chapter I want
to expand on the role of questions and offer a possible format for
asking narrative questions. In doing so, I am not providing a
formula or technique, but offering a process of questioning for
narrative conversation. Formulating good questions is difficult but
essential in narrative pastoral conversations. It is always easier to
give a good answer than to ask a good question. Answers give
power to the one who answers. Open-ended questions with the
motive to learn empower the one of whom the question is asked. To
ask well-phrased questions in the right way at the best time requires
much patience and wisdom. And yet, the only way to gain understanding of a subject is to ask insightful questions.

In pastoral conversations, questions do far more than help
counselees tell their stories. They act as mirrors to stimulate further
reflection. They create new experiences that would not otherwise
have happened. They lead to new understandings. As Hans Georg

Gadamer wrote, "To reach an understanding in a dialogue is not merely putting oneself forward and successfully asserting one's own view, but being transformed into a communion in which we do not remain what we were. [23]

During our school years we were expected to produce the right answers to questions our teachers asked. Studying under that kind of pressure helped us accumulate knowledge, but did little to prepare us for listening to stories told during conversations. Nor did it help us formulate judicious questions to ask people when they would tell us their stories. In pastoral conversations the right kinds of questions lead to the development of a larger story than the one originally told. This, in turn, leads to even greater understanding. Good questions do far more than help us discover hidden information. "This is the reason," said Gadamer, "why understanding is always more than re-creating someone else's meaning. Questions open up the possibilities of meaning, and thus what is meaningful passes into one's own thinking on the subject." [24]

In narrative pastoral conversations we listen to stories, not merely to hear a reproduction of what happened at one point in time, but to engage in a productive activity of story creation. We are doing something far more important than understanding what someone else believes to be true. Our work is more than helping others see their story from different perspectives. What we do is to help recreate the story, bring it from the past tense to the present as faithfully as possible, especially aspects of the story that may have been privileged before the present conversation. It is important to suspend judgment and honestly desire to discover a broader and greater depth to the story.

When we ask questions in our narrative conversations, we may learn something that we chose not to know until it was told to us, usually in the form of a story. Although we learn many things about the other person during our conversation, we may deliberately choose not to guess or make assumptions about a certain aspect of the story.

Good conversationalists are respectful listeners who seldom change the subject except to help stay with the plot of the main story. Nor do they ask questions that will embarrass the other party. The right to ask personal questions is granted only as trust and rapport develop between all parties in the conversation.

We need to be careful about the kinds of questions we ask, of whom we ask them, and how and when we ask them. Questions are indirect requests. They are a call to action—action that leads to experience. If a question (viewed as a call to action) is seen as a criticism, the conversation takes a dead-end turn into defensive responses and, ultimately, termination.

Similarly, questions that highlight problems and incompetencies create dislike of the questioner. A conversation as social interaction can be either enhanced or harmed by questions. Therefore, they should not be asked too frequently or intensely, or they can shut down the sharing. Questions need to communicate a caring interest in the other person's life; they should be asked in a respectful manner that emphasizes strengths, competencies and surprises, rather than dwelling on weaknesses, faults and failures.

During my pastoral counseling training I was taught to mostly listen and give occasional empathic responses to the thoughts and feelings of persons counseling with me. Asking questions was considered intrusive and likely to lead someone to a predetermined response. Years later I discovered that questions asked with respect and genuine interest in the narrative life of a counselee were appreciated. Now I am discovering the power of questions in developing life stories as we co-author those stories together. Good questions are an integral and essential aspect of effective narrative conversation.[25]

I've discovered that when counselees have fixed opinions about the stories they tell, my questions can turn their stories toward a more creative and fluid narrative. Insightful questions widen the perspective on the story. Instead of a one-dimensional view, the counselees begin to see a whole world of story creation possibilities. These questions, coupled with empathic responses, demonstrate caring interest in those telling their stories. This in turn creates a willingness to explore larger meanings for the stories. Questions that bring out the subtexts offer an invitation to re-author parts of the story that would otherwise have been overlooked; they may also reveal perspectives not before considered but told in answer to the questions.[26]

In my counseling experience, I have observed that the more I think I really know a person, the fewer questions I ask. I now try to remind myself to be careful about being too informed by my own opinions. And, of course I do not want to offend by asking questions before I have keenly listened to the counselee. Respectful conversational questions lead to the unfolding of stories as they are being narrated. When I take a not-knowing attitude, I am still in a learning mode where new possibilities for experiences are created as the stories unfold.

When I refuse to be dominated by my own assumptions, expert opinions, psychological knowledge and accumulated wisdom, I do not try to fix people and their problems, even when being urged to do so by the narrator of the stories. Instead, I find myself carefully listening to the unfolding narrative, just as I would watch the dawn revealing the light of a new day. As I truly care for both the narrator and the stories, I rediscover that being heard is more helpful to the narrator than my opinions.

Expertise in narrative pastoral conversation consists not in knowing the answers to people's problems, but in the quality of listening and questioning that aid in authoring and reauthoring the stories. This implies that verbal responses come as much as possible in the language of metaphors and analogies of the counselees. As much as possible, I use key words, phrases, symbols, expressions and stories that come from the counselees. I try to speak their language instead of using my own favorite ways of thinking and speaking.

This means that my questions will not be of a rhetorical nature, having predetermined answers. Nor will they be Socratic, intending to teach or lead to a correct answer.[27] The purpose of the questions is to create new possibilities probably not thought of before by either party in the conversation. As the relationship develops, other thoughts, feelings and actions continue to be created as the story unfolds into more hopeful possibilities.

Unlike traditional pastoral counseling, narrative pastoral conversations do not focus primarily on feelings or on the interpersonal relationship but on the expansion of the stories told by the counselees to include elements previously excluded. Feelings are not neglected; rather, they are included into the larger stories.

Interpersonal relationships are enhanced through storied conversations. As the stories are reconstructed by attentive listening, empathic responses, and careful questions designed to bring out missing parts, the counselees relive in the present moment experiences from the past that have the potential of affective expression. New meanings and additional resources for dealing with the problem aspects of the stories are then integrated into the narrative.

Anna's Narrative

As Anna told her story about the sudden and unexpected departure from her home country when she was ten, her words sounded rehearsed, as though they had been told many times. She was reporting a traumatic life experience that dramatically changed her life and her family relationships. As she recounted basic information, I listened for several minutes, then asked some narrative questions to get a sense of what it was like for her as a ten-year-old. As she responded, we explored with words the landscape where she had lived before the sudden exile from her home. She took great delight in describing her life growing up with a caring, extended family in a tropical environment. These words sounded unrehearsed, freshly created for this particular time.

She told me about the important characters in her life story, especially her beloved grandmother who served as her primary care giver. When I asked her if her grandmother immigrated when she did, tears flowed from her eyes as she told me she never saw her grandmother again. Because her family left secretly in the middle of the night to avoid the military police, she was not allowed to bid farewell to her grandmother. When I asked what she told herself about this experience, profuse tears spilled over as she grieved for the first time the loss of her grandmother, a loss that became permanent when the grandmother died a few years later.

Anna started the conversation by telling me a story. Soon we were revising her old, often told story and co-creating a new story that included the losses sustained by the move from one country to another. Her story became our story. At another session we expanded the chapters of her story when I asked how she could best honor the memory of her grandmother. This initiated a series of beautiful letters and poems written to her deceased grandmother. Anna discovered her writing talent as she crafted a story of redemption from her pain.

Imagining Your Story

Future-oriented questions carry the potential of creating feelings about a more hopeful future. No one question can do all of this, but the narrative process of questioning around the plot of the story is as important as the story itself. [28]

Imagination and storytelling go together. Each time a story is told, a new imaginative creation and recreation of the story takes place. This doesn't mean that the old story was false. Neither does it mean that the new story is true. There is always more and less to a story than can be told at one time.

Questions stimulate the imaginative capacity of the storyteller to reconstruct and re-author the story. Narrative pastoral conversations evolve slowly, and a detailed, concrete, individual life story can be stimulated from a position of not-knowing and a desire to learn.[29] This is a completely different approach from the position of a pastor who claims to have expert knowledge for resolving people's problems.

It is important to remember that no questions are free from value meanings and implications. Secular counselors ask value-laden questions just as often as pastors do. I try to be as informed as possible about the values behind my questions, because I can't help but be influenced by my Christian beliefs, the biblical stories, and the culture of the communities of faith where I minister.

Asking questions in narrative pastoral conversations can be unsettling because the answers are undetermined. They are waiting to be created. As Gadamer says, "The question takes priority over the answer because only a person who has questions can have knowledge."[30] The hardest thing to acknowledge is that I do not know, and cannot know, unless I ask questions. Neither can other parties in the conversation know as much as they need to know unless good questions are an integral part of the exchange. Questions usually lead to more questions and more lively conversation. The parties are transformed in a meaningful dialogue that goes far beyond the original thought that stimulated the conversation.

In narrative conversations, I want to think like a novelist who looks at the world as a question. Good questions, like good novels, are best known by the answers received from the story of the struggle with the question. When someone asks to talk with me about a personal problem, I think of myself as a curious researcher without a predetermined hypothesis, not trying to prove or disprove anything, but hoping to know the person and the story this person wants to tell. The better I can suppress a desire to be helpful, the more the person is helped. I try to respectfully get to know the person by showing interest through asking questions about the key elements of the story in order to help create possibilities and new versions of a more hopeful life. Asking good questions at the proper time, and in a tactful manner, requires sensitivity to the needs of the counselee and a love for storying conversations.

Questions Format

Borrowing from White and Epston are some narrative pastoral questions. Do not think of them as formula, but as examples of the process and kinds of questions that I might ask in the first or second counseling session. I do not ask them every time. Neither do I start asking them until I listen with empathic responses to the opening story of the counselee, for at least fifteen to thirty minutes.

In the blank space place the name of the problem chosen by the counselee. Short, non-pathological, user-friendly names are the best. I usually recommend to my students that they first use these questions as a spiritual exercise by choosing a specific issue in their lives that they need to face, with the help of God. After selecting the issue and giving it a specific name, go through the questions slowly and prayerfully.

Preparing to use questions in counseling . . .
- Establish a relationship through the use of listening skills.
- Work from a position of respect for the counselee, through acceptance, openness and hopeful expectation.
- Use a reflecting position to facilitate listening to the counselee and quieting one's own desire to talk.
- The person is more important than the story. The story is more important than the problem. Help the counselee tell the story.

Discovering and naming the problem . . .
- Remember that the problem is the problem, not the person.
- Think of the problem as a thing or a spiritual force.
- Talk about the problem as an active agent in the life of the person(s).
- Use the metaphor of the counselee.
- If you could give a name to the main problem that is affecting you, what would you call it?
- From what you have said, could we call the problem _____?

Exploring the effects of the problem . . .
- Expand the story by exploring the effects of the problem in several areas of the person's life, especially where it is causing the most pain.

How does_____affect you?
What does_____get you to do?
What does_____take you from?
How does_____ affect others?
How long has_____been with you?
What enjoyment has this problem taken from you?

Searching for frequency and exceptions . . .
- It is important to discover the prevalency of the problem.
- Exceptions are the leverage for overcoming the power of the problem.

- Problems create tunnel vision. Expand the story around the problem where it is not present.

Is _____ with you all of the time?
What percent of the time is it not present?
What are you doing when is not running your life?
How do others relate to you then?
How could you increase this percentage of freedom from_____?
When _____ tries to trick you into doing it again, how do you escape its power?
Are you pleased when you refuse to let it control you?
Were there times in the past when you did not have this problem?
Do you remember how it started?

Developing the preferred story . . .
- Ask about the desires, values, intentions, goals and dreams for the future that are directly related to the problem.
- Look for strengths, commitment and competencies.
Open space for re-authoring.

How will you know that you have conquered_____?
As you gain successes, how do you think others will know this?
When you live by your values regarding_____, what skills will you be using?
What will your victory over_____ tell others about you?
How do you think they will respond to you?
What does this tell you about yourself?
What surprises would you expect?

Extending the plot of the story into the future . . .
- Develop a new more hopeful, solution-oriented future story.
- Name the counter-plot to the problem story.
- Use the miracle question.
- Circulate the story to a wider audience.

Putting_____behind you, what would you call this new life?

Suppose that while you sleep tonight, God performs a miracle and you find that_____is no longer with you when you awake tomorrow: what would that be like for you?

What will you be doing when you demonstrate that the miracle happened?

Who would notice the change?

Who would be happy for you?

Who would be skeptical?

How could you keep the miracle?

Have parts of this miracle already started to happen?

How do you think things will be for you in two weeks, months, years?

Instead of_____, what would you call this new life?

What does this tell you about yourself?

How can you use this to help you confront the problem you have talked about with me?

What kinds of decisions do you need to make?

Using faith resources . . .

- Look and listen for Bible story analogies.
- Ask what the counselee has been praying for, and how others are praying for him/her.
- Ask what you, as the counselor, should pray for in relationship to_____.

Does your story remind you of anyone in the Bible?

Do you mind if I share a Bible story/saying that your story brought to my mind?

Have you been praying about this problem? How? How long?

Are other people praying for you?

Have there been some answers?

How will you know the prayers have been answered?

What should I pray for concerning this problem?

Will you tell me when and how the prayers are answered?

These suggested questions should not be used as a formula for all counseling problems, but they can help a counselor create questions for examining a problem from a larger perspective. The story of Pastor Ken in chapter 6 will demonstrate this model of reflective questioning.

Chapter Six

Creative Storying

"To reach an understanding on a dialogue is not merely
a matter of putting oneself forward and asserting one's own point
of view, but being transformed into a communion in which we do
not remain what we were."

Hans-George Gadamer

According to the article "Thinking Like a Genius" by Michael Michalko, people who are considered geniuses do not have especially high IQ'S. What they do have is a high level of creativity, which is not the same thing as intelligence. People can be intelligent and not creative, or creative and not very intelligent. Michalko claims that studies on outstanding contributors to science and the arts show they have certain things in common.

The outstanding characteristic of creative people is that they are productive, rather than reproductive, thinkers. When confronted with a problem they do not settle for something in the past that once worked for them. That would be reproductive thinking which assumes that because something worked at one time in one place, it will work again in this new situation. Productive thinkers look for new and unique approaches.[31]

Reproductive Thinking   ·

While productive thinking uses the given story or situation to create new ideas, reproductive thinking only retells the story or seeks to relate facts about the situation. Applying the difference between productive and reproductive thinking in counseling means that the reproductive counselor hears about a problem and then mentally goes to a repertoire of solutions that worked in similar situations. This could be a situation in the counselor's own life, a previously known person, or a technique, which is now used to help in the new situation. Reproductive thinking works well for technical problems that can be repeated over and over the same way, but not very well for personal and relational problems. Technical answers are best limited to technical problems. They seldom work with personal and relational issues.

As a narrative conversationalist I sometimes use reproductive thinking when I ask counselees to think about a time when they faced difficult situations and to tell me what worked well then. After they make a connection with a familiar action, they can now transfer the knowledge or successful technique from one problem to another. Not much creativity is taking place here, because this is still reproductive thinking.

Productive Thinking

From reading Michalko's article I learned that to shift from reproductive to productive thinking requires a new way of looking at issues. Rather than returning to past knowledge or seeking the cause of the problem in the past, the counselor now thinks creatively about the many ways the problem could be viewed. Starting with a not-knowing-but-wanting-to-learn attitude I may ask, "How many different ways could I look at this story to find a more acceptable ending? What questions would most facilitate productive thinking?" This stimulates productive creativity. Older and sometimes workable solutions are put on the back burner, and new ways to think about the problem become the major focus of the conversation.

Einstein was once asked what was the difference between him and the average person. "He said that, if you asked the average person to find a needle in a haystack, the person would stop when he or she found a needle. He, on the other hand, would tear through the entire haystack looking for all the possible needles." [32] Einstein was considered a genius because he believed that problems are not solved by using the same way of thinking and doing that which created the problem in the first place. He used productive thinking to find new ways to look at old information. This implies asking new kinds of questions instead of looking for answers from old information.

In a conversation with Paul, my youngest son about his wood carving art, I asked if he approached a block of rough wood with a picture in mind of what he wanted to create. His response was immediate. He said, "Never would I do that. It wouldn't be art if I knew in advance what the grains of wood had to offer. We have to work together to discover the final form the carving is to take. I never know in advance what will come out of the wood." Paul's art is creatively productive, rather than reproductive.

Narrative Productive Thinking

Narrative pastoral conversationalists try new ways of looking at the story and facilitates, mostly through questions to create productive thinking about the counselee's problem-saturated story. This means helping the counselee's search for the exceptions to the problem and consider both the least obvious as well as the most likely solutions. Doing this in a natural flow of conversation encourages productive thinking about problems in different ways. It's a mental trial-and-error scenario creation of future possibilities.

I believe most people get stuck in their problems because they use reproductive rather than productive thinking. The loss of creative thinking can be as much of the problem as the problem itself. Sometimes I ask counselees who are stuck in a problem, "What do you imagine will happen if you keep doing in the future what you have been doing in the past?" Usually they have little trouble imagining increased pain and destructiveness. Some are like drivers who do not realize that once stuck in the sand the worst thing you can do is push harder on the accelerator.

I'm not suggesting that we teach creativity to counselees; rather, I believe in mutually restorying a problem with the judicious use of open-ended narrative questions to help rediscover a creative way of looking at the problem. I've found productive thinking to be more effective in helping counselees get unstuck from their problem. The narrative pastoral conversationalist is not the one with most of the answers or the latest techniques for change, but the one who practices by modeling and stimulating productive thinking in counselees.

Leonardo de Vinci believed that to gain knowledge of a problem, he had to reconsider it in many different ways. He felt that the first way he looked at a problem was too biased toward his usual way of seeing things. He would restructure his problem by looking at it from one perspective, move to another perspective and still another. With each move his understanding would deepen and he would begin to understand the essence of the problem. In this way he could overcome the common bias of assuming that there is one right answer to a problem. The best of many possible solutions is much more effective.[33]

Conversations employing productive thinking take more time at first but will save time later. Helping people develop creative, solution-oriented skills for dealing with problems encourages them to discover their own solutions when faced with new problems. I enjoy this approach much more than thinking about problems to be solved or predetermined solutions to be found. I find myself energized by a productively creative and focused conversation. This requires the use of the imagination, something often found lacking in counselees.

Productive Conversation in a Pastoral Visit

In the following story about a pastoral visit, we will see how one pastor used a creative narrative approach in a conversation. What follows are his reflections upon both the story and his own thought processes as the story unfolded. I have re-created the story from a conversation with Pastor Ken. You will see how he participated in a narrative storying conversation with the use of a not-knowing but wanting-to-learn attitude and the strategic use of questions.

The story is narrated on two levels. One level is the conversation between Pastor Ken and the couple he was visiting. The other level is a meta-conversation—or conversation about the conversation—by the pastor to himself as he reflects on his internal experience during the visit.

Ten minutes into the pastoral visit with Diane and Tim Taylor, the subject of worrying about the future came up. Diane told Pastor Ken that she was concerned with her husband's habit of worrying about things that seldom happened. She said this was creating a lot of sleepless nights for him and unhappiness in the home. She asked, "Do you know of anything we can do about this problem? We have enough things to be concerned about, and I don't want to listen to his constant talk about things that could happen but never do." Immediately, Pastor Ken realized the pastoral visit was shifting onto a more serious level.

Feeling somewhat uncomfortable with Diane talking critically about her husband in his presence, Ken looked at Tim and asked, "Do you have a tendency to worry and, if so, is this as much of a concern to you as it is to your wife?" Tim tried to minimize Diane's concern, but soon admitted that it had become a problem in their relationship.

Ken asked, "Your wife wants to talk about this problem. Do you mind if all three of us talk about it together?" Tim gave his permission.

As their pastor, Ken had several decisions to make as to how they would proceed with this conversation. Several thoughts went rapidly through his mind as he tried to develop a pastoral response to their concerns. The first idea that came to him was to be very direct by giving them some advice about worry and ways to overcome it. He had frequently used the advice approach in the early years of his ministry, but decided against doing so now because it had sometimes gotten him into trouble with people he tried to help. Either they did not follow his advice, or they blamed him when it didn't work. With the hindsight of experience he disciplined his tongue against telling them what he thought they ought to do to overcome the problem. He was thankful that he was growing beyond the need to claim power over the lives of other persons through assuming the role of the expert and telling them how to resolve personal problems. Also, he remembered resenting people who glibly tried to explain things they did not fully understand and then tell him what he ought to do.

The next approach Ken considered was offering comfort from the Bible or by a prayer. He dismissed this idea as being both premature and somewhat superficial for the concerns of this couple. They would have opportunity to pray with clearer discernment at the end of his visit.

He paid attention to the feelings in his body and realized how nervous he was by being confronted without warning with an issue that deserved a pastoral response. He too had struggled with the tendency to worry about his ministry. It would be easier and safer for him to lead the conversation in a more comfortable direction, perhaps telling them some practical things they might try to control worry. It would be more comfortable to lead a conversation from his own frame of reference than to enter the uncertainty of the moment. This would relieve his anxiety, but was not likely to help them.

Fortunately, Pastor Ken remembered something he learned during his training for ministry. He recalled that listening to people is the initial and most important thing a pastor can do to help someone. Though it did not come easily to him, he was discovering some of the advantages of the ministry of listening and was learning to control his tendency to talk too much.

Ken thought he was a fairly good conversationalist. He enjoyed humor and kept up with current events, but he also knew of his tendency to dominate conversations. Because of this he was attempting to become a better listener by practicing it in conversations of a more serious nature, especially when members of his church asked him for help with personal concerns.

Coming out of this quick internal reflection while he listened to Diane, Ken decided he needed to develop a better understanding of their problem and should not rush to find answers. "Tell me more about this problem," he asked. He listened to each of them and thought how important it was not to make either of them the focus of the problem. He tried to keep the conversation focused on the problem, rather than on either partner in the marriage; to do otherwise could complicate their relationship. He wondered how this problem, developed in the intimate context of their marriage, could have become such a controlling part of their relationship.

Ken knew that Tim and Diane needed to provide their own name for the problem, rather than his tagging it with a psychological diagnostic name. Naming a problem is important for the person who lives with it, because naming provides a sense of personal agency over the problem. He asked, "Could you help me by giving a short name for the problem we have been talking about?"

At first this request seemed strange to them, but after discussing what they would call the problem, Tim said, "Why don't we call it 'worry.' Is that short enough?" They laughed and agreed that this would be a good name.

Ken realized that "worry" had been with Tim and Diane for some time and that it was affecting their relationship in a negative way, but he did not want their conversation to become problem focused. He preferred that they find some solutions together after exploring their story about worry. Nor did he want to focus on the causes of the problem, for this would squander valuable time trying to create understanding of the cause without finding solutions. In his early ministry he thought he needed to find root causes of problems by digging into the past. He knew that he was not an expert in the use of psychological language, though this was the way educated people in his culture talked about personal problems.

Some months earlier it had dawned on Ken that figuring out what causes a problem does not solve the problem. It was a good approach to problems with material things in order to find out what was wrong and then try to fix them, but it was not an effective way to work with people. He valued his pastoral relationship with Tim and Diane and did not want to spoil it by treating them as objects to be fixed. He viewed them as persons created in the image of God with gifts and graces from God to defeat worry. They had experience with marriage and had overcome many problems before worry took up residence in their home. He wanted to use their ideas in finding solutions rather than to focus on their weaknesses.

He hoped to continue in a conversational manner without using words that would place him in the role of the person with expert knowledge. If Tim had a medical problem, he needed to see a physician with proper training to diagnose and prescribe medication. Ken did wonder if Tim was depressed, but decided against approaching him as a depressed person. Ken remembered that he was helping them with the problem called "worry," not Tim as a sick person or Diane as an anxious person, because she was upset about worry dominating their relationship. Ken understood worry as a form of bondage in Tim's life that also affected his wife and, in turn, their relationship. He wanted to be their pastor and help them overcome this bondage to worry.

In his search to find a new approach to helping people overcome the problems that oppressed them, Ken had discovered the power of stories. This approach did not surprise Ken when he remembered how accustomed he was to using stories in his preaching and teaching ministry. He was familiar with the stories of the Bible and their power to influence the lives of people who read and hear them. Jesus frequently used stories in His ministry. Until recently it had never occurred to Ken that using a narrative method for pastoral conversation could help transform lives. He had started experimenting with this new approach to counseling and pastoral care by helping people tell their stories to see if this would turn their lives toward a more positive direction.

Ken soon discovered more than a new technique of counseling. Focusing on stories was a new way of thinking about how people know and believe what they do. For him this was like shifting from one way of viewing reality to another. The implications of these changes were not clear at first, but he felt the excitement of discovering a new and natural way of relating to people, plus a conversational style of counseling. He realized that when people converse with each other they tell stories, so one day he asked himself, "If people communicate with each other primarily through telling stories, why not use this same approach when counseling?" Little did he realize the many ways a narrative orientation to conversations would change his way of thinking about people and about counseling.

Ken decided to take an unknowing, or curious attitude in his conversation with Tim and Diane. Instead of telling them what he thought they ought to do, or to tell his own stories about worry, he shifted from a position of certainty to a position of faith. He was learning to live with the mystery of faith rather than hide behind his understanding. He became very interested in listening to them tell their stories of worry but without imposing preconceived ideas on how they would find a solution. If he helped them expand their own story to include some parts that they had overlooked, he hoped that Diane and Tim would discover the solution for themselves.

Ken asked Diane and Tim to tell him more about "worry". "How has 'worry' affected your lives and your relationship?" He listened to their story about "worry" as he would follow a story in a book. He paid special attention to the basic elements of a narrative; the plot with character, setting and action told with a beginning, a middle and an end. He anticipated that their story would be an artistic recreation of the life of worry, rather than just a factual recounting of events. Since they were the primary authors of their narrative, he would function as a co-author with them by virtue of the questions he asked, when he asked them, and how he asked them. Their conversation carried the potential of creating a new version of the story about "worry".

As Tim told his story of "worry", Ken let them know that he was listening from the heart, by occasional empathic, reflective statements as he followed their lead. They told him more and more about their life of worry and how it had come to dominate Tim's thoughts and spoiled many of their conversations. Ken followed their account as closely as he would a good mystery story. He asked questions about how "worry" convinced them to act as they did and what they thought about this. He was intensely interested in the many ways "worry" had influenced their lives. "Worry" had taken on the role of a third character in their relationship, somewhat in the same way a child becomes the center of attention in a family.

More important, Ken wanted to hear the parts of the story related to their resistance to the control of "worry". He asked what they had done to control or get rid of "worry". Diane told about how she tried to reason with her husband, to keep him busy, to get him to read something beside the bad things reported in the newspapers. Lately, she found herself getting angry with her husband and avoiding talking with him. She was concerned with their future life together if this continued much longer. Suddenly, she said, "I guess I have seen Tim as the problem. I never thought about 'worry' itself being the problem. I would like to keep my husband, but I sure want 'worry' to get out of our house."

Tim told about his efforts to defeat "worry". Many times he tried to talk himself out of worrying only to have it return again and again. He tried to sort out the actual problems and do what he could about them so they would not add to his worrying. He even tried reading the Bible more, especially verses that encouraged a positive outlook on life. He tried thinking positive thoughts, but soon found himself submerged in worrying again. The most effective way he escaped worry was to work all the time. This gave temporary relief, but it also left him fatigued most of the time, thus giving him something else to worry about. Tim told several mini-stories about his battle with worrying.

The time for the visit was slipping away and Ken wanted their conversation to include stories about their strengths and competencies in confronting other problems in life that they had overcome. He thought that focusing too much on the details of the problem with worry would keep their attention on weaknesses more than their strengths. He asked them if they had confronted other problems and were able to overcome them. Both Tim and Diane told about times when they faced problems and how they overcame them. From the looks on their faces Ken knew they were recovering some of the confidence that worry was taking away from them. He asked, "Can you think of how transferring some of these skills in dealing with other problems might help you get 'worry' out of your home?" They offered no immediate response to his question, but Ken knew they were reflecting on these positive experiences in a way that could help them with their present concern. They promised to think about this and recall some of the skills they used in managing other major problems during their marriage.

Ken needed to leave soon for another appointment, but he did not want to stop with the story of worry in the middle of the plot.

He could make a follow-up visit, but more of the story needed to be developed before he left. He resisted the temptation to cut their story off by making suggestions about things they could do to overcome worry. This would mean that he would take over as the primary author of their story rather than helping them develop a more hopeful story for the future when worry no longer controlled their relationship. He did not want them to become dependent upon him as their answer man. He wanted to be their pastor, not their problem solver. He believed they could rely on their relationship with God to help them. He asked if they had prayed about this problem. When they said they had been praying, but not about this particular problem, he asked if each one would tell him what he or she was accustomed to ask for in prayer. He was not surprised to learn that they had never thought about asking God to help them overcome the worry problem. "Think about what you want God to do for you in relation to this problem called 'worry'," he said.

After a short discussion about this prayer, he asked some future-oriented questions to see if this would help them expand their story and help them form a vision of life without worry in control. He asked, "What difference would it make for each of you and your relationship if after you go to bed tonight a miracle takes place while you are sleeping and God answers your prayers about "worry"? When you wake up tomorrow worry is expelled from your home. Worry no longer uses up your time and spoils your peace of mind or your marriage. He is gone for good. What would life be like for you? What would be different?" These questions surprised Tim and Diane. Before this conversation they had never considered that their story could contain liberation from worry. Excitement and laughter flowed from their mouths as they described their lives without the control of "worry." They expanded the plot of the story to include an ending that previously had never been imagined. Some glimmers of light started to shine through the darkness. Their "worry" story was headed in a new direction. They were visibly excited about this possibility. They laughed together as they talked about life after worry left their home. They were like parents talking about the enjoyable things they would do when all the children left home.

As Ken listened to this conversation about freedom from the problem of worry, he knew that Diane and Tim still had lots of work to do, but he also saw they had a new sense of hope that would help them create a future without worry controlling their marriage. With hope from a story vision of freedom, their lives would no longer be trapped in the old story. This was much more than a new way of thinking about the problem. Developing faith in a future without worry was an essential step in taking action against "worry".

Ken realized again that the story is more important than the problem. Problem stories surround the problem and direct the life of the problem. This does not mean that the problems are unreal. Neither are stories unreal. Problems are best faced with a clear vision of life after the problem is no longer in control. The difference comes in changes to the ways of looking at the problem, no matter how real it may be to those who live with it. Without a story of hope that includes life without "worry", the problem story controls the plot.

Ken went on to strengthen their confidence in the possibility of change by asking Diane and Tim to imagine sharing the good news about their new freedom over worry. "Who would be happy for you" he asked, "if they heard about your defeat of "worry"? Who would be most disappointed, or skeptical?" He asked questions about what others would think and talk about when their prayers were answered. Ken listened to their creative ideas as they imagined how others might respond to their story of freedom over "worry".

Ken warned them that uninvited guests such as "worry" are not easily convinced to leave, let alone stay away. When forced to leave, like insects, they start looking for opportunities to return, invited or not. Ken was preparing Diane and Tim for the danger of letting down their guard, now that they were feeling better about their ability to do something about the problem. He asked them to think about ways they thought "worry" would try to get back into their home. They recalled some of the familiar strategies "worry" had used to control their lives. Talking about this increased their resolve not to continue with their old patterns of relating with each other as they did when "worry" controlled their relationship.

It was time to pray. Ken's prayer for Tim and Diane was much more meaningful now that he had taken the time to listen to their concerns. He had helped them find their own solutions in the form of a new story. They were much better informed about the issue of "worry". It was up to them to struggle to develop the new story of life without "worry" controlling their home life. They sensed a new direction they wanted to go. He prayed that God would strengthen their faith and help them to live free of the control of the problem of "worry".

Tim and Diane felt respected by their pastor. His questions helped them name and describe the story of their problem. The conversational manner of talking with everyday words encouraged them to think about the problem in more hopeful ways. No longer was Tim the problem person because he worried. Tim and Diane now saw the problem as extraneous to their personhood. They were empowered and ready to work together to overcome it.

Before leaving, Pastor Ken said he would call them soon to find out how they were overcoming this problem and defeating "worry." The next day he wrote a letter to Tim and Diane to affirm their decision to defeat worry. In the letter he reviewed the key issues in their conversation and told them that he was praying for them and looked forward to talking with them again in the near future.

Chapter Seven

Narrative Conversations in Times of Crisis

"Never waste a good crisis."

Most good short stories or novels are about crises in the lives of the main characters. In a similar way, many pastoral conversations are about present or past crisis experiences in the lives of counselees.

I can think of no more important occasion for using carefully chosen narrative pastoral questions than in times of grief. The best way to help family members is to host the telling of their stories about the life of the deceased. Everyone closely connected to the deceased person has an important story to share. Telling stories about someone who has died is a way of honoring the deceased, coping with grief, and creating a new sense of meaning, purpose and closure.

In narrative pastoral conversations, I become a part of the story as I help others share their stories. I function somewhat like a director of an unfolding drama where all the characters act out roles as they participate in the story of one whose ending can now be told. Narrative questions do much more than gather information about their relationship with the deceased. As a director of the drama, I'm generating new experiences to form a meaningful and redemptive story, even in the midst of suffering. Reflexive questions invite family and friends to restory their own lives in light of the new events.

Before the funeral service, I try to find some private time to gather the grieving family in a semicircle around the casket. I call this "the horseshoe." Then I ask each one to share a story they want to remember about the deceased family member. At first this may be painful, but soon almost everyone has something to say, often something humorous. I've discovered that people who share stories about important events directly related to the deceased usually have less difficulty with the grieving process. Saying, "I remember when" from a memory about the deceased gives a sense of permanence that death cannot take away. When I officiate at the funeral, I use some of these stories to put into perspective the life of the person who died and also to take some of the sting out of death.

Questions asked of grieving people do not change the situation, but they do generate a more meaningful story for future retelling. I try to make sure I am in tune with the person(s) with whom I am talking before asking questions. I want to help them express what is happening with them at that moment and also help them put into words the meaning of this experience. I am aware of the psychological dynamics of grief and am careful not to take away from the significance of the death for each person. Hosting their stories communicates respect for storyteller and for the deceased.

Out of concern for persons in crisis, trauma, or grieving, after carefully listening to their story, I may ask narrative questions to help them verbalize the experiences. Some possible questions are:

- What were your reactions when you first heard about this?
- What have you been telling yourself about this person or situation?
- What is the worst thing about this for you?
- What has been going on since you got the news?
- What kinds of questions are you asking yourself about this situation?

- How have you managed to this point?
- How are you coping?
- Have you ever been through something like this? How did you cope then?
- What kind of assistance do you need to help you get through this?
- How can I best pray for you?

Restorying Early Losses

In conversations about a previous loss, I take a different approach to narrative questions. I call this "encapsulated grief," because the loss has never been grieved enough to bring release and healing. However, it is never too late to find closure.

Annabel Lee is the beloved of the narrator in Edgar Allen Poe's famous poem of the same name. In it he tells the story of his love for a young woman—of her beauty and of how he dreams of her night after night. His precious, beautiful, loving bride is long since dead, having been stolen away from him by the chilling, killing, cruel wind of death, which came by stealth in the night when she was hardly more than a child.

> *For the moon never beams without bringing me dreams*
> *Of the beautiful Annabel Lee;*
> *And the stars never rise but I see the bright eyes*
> *Of the beautiful Annabel Lee . . .*

The poet is refusing to re-author the story of his beloved to include releasing her to be dead and gone. She has been buried, yet she's still alive and controlling a part of his life. He tells us that still, to the day he writes, the moon never shines and the stars never come out but that he thinks of his Annabel Lee lying cold in her sepulcher down by the sea. He expresses rage at the jealous angels who have stolen his only angel; thus, the poem is filled with his dark, depressing grief. Most of all, he makes it clear that he will never let go of his love, even though she is dead. Since he refuses to let her go, he continues to feel the kind of grief that will not reach resolution, for he does not want it to be over. She is being held in limbo in his heart; she is gone from him, but not all the way gone. She is dead, but not totally departed. She lives on in his heart and dreams.

The poem is a good example of ungrieved and incomplete stories of grief: the depression, anger, brooding, reliving and rehashing, blaming, and even denial that the loved one is dead and gone.

Unrequited Love

One of the most enduring losses is the death of a fiancé and the subsequent pain of unrequited love. Kay met her fiancé, Ben, during orientation week in their freshman year of college. Both were popular and talented students. They became engaged at Christmas of their sophomore year and everyone predicted success and happiness for this beautiful couple. Then disaster struck on an icy mountain road where Ben was killed in an automobile accident. Kay's family, friends, and classmates surrounded her with such affection and concern that she had little time to think about what her loss meant to her emotionally. Because of her deepening depression, she made excuses to stay away from friends. She did agree to go out on some dates, just to have something to do, but she was unable to have a good time. She usually refused to go out with a young man more than once. Her relationships became tentative and she lost interest in living. She went through the motions of studying and somehow managed to get by in school.

After attending a lecture I gave on death and dying, Kay asked to talk with me. When she came for an appointment, she wanted to talk about some of the symptoms of the "walking dead" I had described in class. She saw for the first time that she had not realized the full impact of Ben's death. But now, she was beginning to identify with some of the stories she had been reading in a counseling book. Her major concern was her lack of responsiveness to other men. When she told me the story surrounding the loss of her fiancé, I asked her to describe her marital status (single, engaged, married, divorced, or widowed). She responded that she was technically single, but she felt widowed.

It soon became evident to her that she had developed a story about her life that included a bond of commitment to Ben that was not broken by his death and burial. As she related the story of the relationship and his tragic death, she wept openly and started the painful process of releasing Ben to his final resting place. When I asked her what it would mean to her when she released herself from the promise to marry Ben, she began to think about a future that did not include him as her life partner. I suggested that she make one last visit with his family to his gravesite to say goodbye to him and all the potential in-laws.

Kay required no intensive counseling. What she needed was to tell her story and receive permission to grieve Ben's loss. A few weeks later she dropped by my office to tell me that she felt much better and looked forward to dating again. Through the restorying of her experience and painful grieving, she was released to create future stories of love and family. Two years later, I received an invitation to her wedding.

Unresolved grief will always be with us unless we have the courage to come to terms with it. The shadow of the deceased follows the soul of the living. When we refuse to face this shadow something in us dies along with our loved one; but when we have the courage to turn towards it we are comforted by and made stronger than we were before the loss. Stories seek their own completion.

Normally, our personal story ends when we die, but we can also die when our story ends. We can become like walking dead persons, when the death of a loved one creates a void of new life-giving stories. The most common loss is the capacity to deeply love another person. Grief stories act as a purging agent to clean out the powerful influence of the personality of the deceased. Then we are free to create new stories and reauthor old ones.

Death Means Loss

Mike was a minister serving on the staff of a large inner city church. One of his responsibilities was to visit the sick in the hospitals. In a peer reflection group that I led, he reported that a young man close to his age was hospitalized with terminal cancer. He said that he found the visits extremely difficult and usually had to leave before completing what he would normally hope to achieve during a visit with a dying patient. He could not understand his emotional reactions to this patient.

When one of his peers asked, "Did you have a close friend during your adolescent years?" Mike replied that his father was a minister and the family frequently moved. However, during his high school years they did stay in one place and he and Jim became buddies. Mike's expression grew animated as he talked about their teenage escapades. Then, suddenly he became very quiet and looked sad.

Someone asked, "What happened to him?"

"Jim was killed while serving in the military and I do not want to talk about him anymore." Mike had never grieved the death of his friend.

Another member of the peer group asked Mike what he and Jim did after graduation from high school. He said that he was drafted and sent to Germany after basic training, but most of his friends were sent to Vietnam.

When someone asked, "How did you learn about Jim's death?" Mike resisted answering, but was encouraged to share what he could with the group. He related that he continued writing to his friend after arriving in Germany, but soon the letters were being returned to him by the military postal system. He thought Jim had been transferred out of his unit. One day as he was packing to go on maneuvers, a letter arrived from his mother with news from home. One of the sentences read, "By the way, did you hear that Jim was killed in a helicopter crash in Vietnam?" When asked about his reaction to the news, Mike said that he had had no time to react, because he had to leave on maneuvers with the troops. He tried to put it out of his mind then, and had made himself not think or talk about Jim since that time.

I wanted to bring this story of the past into the present. I folded a piece of paper like a letter and handed it to Mike and asked him to open it and read the same sentence he read years earlier when he first got the news about Jim's death. Mike went through the motion of unfolding the paper. Then, as he visualized the death notice, he suddenly became aware of the loss of his buddy, a death that had not been grieved. It was as fresh as the day he first heard of the loss. His face showed shock and disbelief, and then he burst into loud, body-wrenching sobs which lasted for twenty to thirty minutes.

When Mike could talk again, he began to tell about his loneliness as a boy and how much having a friend in high school had meant to him. He went in and out of his sobbing as he talked. We sat with him and helped him story his grief. At the end of our meeting, I suggested that the story would not be complete without a memorial service for Jim at the gravesite.

The following Sunday afternoon in a pouring rain, we gathered with him in the cemetery to hold the memorial service. Mike's appearance was that of a person whose close friend had died only three days previously. The days and weeks that followed were difficult for him. He felt weak from drained emotions caused by intense grief. Through the support of his wife and his peers, he began to restory his life—without his friend Jim, but with the capacity to feel close to other people. He reported to the group that his anxiety in visiting the young man who was dying from cancer had disappeared. He now looked forward to the visits as he walked through the "valley of the shadow of death" with the patient. Through reauthoring the story of his own grief, he could listen to the stories of his dying parishioner.

Comfort Comes Through Mourning

Kay's and Mike's stories show a widespread and unfortunate approach that many people take toward the loss of a loved one, especially loss through death: They try not to grieve. Or, perhaps they allow themselves to grieve for a few hours, a few days, or a few weeks. But, since life must go on, they resume their normal lives before they have reauthored their grief stories.

Grief may be imaged as a wound. When we love another

person, we gradually invest more and more of ourselves in them so that our stories are intertwined. Should our loved one die, it is as though part of us—the part which we have invested in the loved one—is torn away. The result is not only the loss of the loved one but a large gaping hole in ourselves. The pain that we feel from this double loss is what makes up grief: feelings of anger, sadness, guilt, fear, rage, denial, loneliness, and depression. The wound is "bleeding." The story is tragically unfinished, ever waiting to continue.

Mike and Kay suffered such losses. Since their wounds had not healed, they continued to suffer from their grief. Their grief was incomplete because their grief story was unfinished. They were unhealed.

In the Gospels Jesus says a very strange thing: "Blessed are they who mourn, for they shall be comforted!" Strange indeed, until we realize that the word "comfort" is an English translation of the Latin words *cum forte*. The loose translation of these two words would be "with strength." But *fortis* in Latin is a specific word, referring to that special kind of courage or strength that makes a good soldier. In this sense strength would be great courage or "toughness." This kind of strong person does not easily frighten and would never again be terrified at the thought of battle, because he or she had already experienced hand-to-hand combat and lived to tell the tale. Comfort would then translate more accurately as "extreme bravery and strength," like that of the seasoned soldier.

"Blessed are they who mourn, for they shall be comforted" means that those who mourn can be happy knowing that in grieving their loss they have become even stronger and braver than before. It is in this sense that we approach the work of grieving. Not to resolve or complete our grief is to be permanently wounded, whereas to heal from our grief is to become stronger than ever. Mourning is a form of healing, a process unto life.

Living with the Dead

The poet who loved Annabel Lee did not know or did not choose the process of healing through deep grief. Between the lines he tells us that he would rather be one of the walking dead, clutching his Annabel Lee, than let go of her and live alone and whole. His grief envelopes him like a perpetual thick fog, blotting out the road ahead.

Refusing the suffering that comes with the restorying process is one way in which we are tempted to avoid grieving; so too is clinging to the lost loved one through vows and promises, tying some aspect or dimension of our present life to the memory or loyalty of the lost one, because we cannot be as close to any new person as we were to the lost loved one. In the case of Mike, denial had been so complete that even he was surprised to discover his grief! That, of course, is what denial achieves: a kind of protection from pain. Unfortunately for us, however, the "protection" does not make grief go away. It only prolongs the hurt and makes the wound fester as we go on living with the dead.

Unmerging from the Dead

To love someone is to invest a part of oneself in them. The very beginning of life is such an experience, in that each one of us begins as part of our mother and for several years after birth are emotionally merged with her. "Unmerging" is painful in the most fundamental sense, even though we must do so in order to be individuals. From that point on, we find it good to be alone and good also to be with those whom we love. When we actually "fall in love," it is much better to be together in love than to be alone. Unmerging in the sense of loss becomes painful, even overwhelming. It is a complete re-authoring of our lives with a future without the one lost. Some of the words we use for "unmerging" when in love reflect this pain: boyfriends and girlfriends call it "breaking up;" married people call it "splitting up." Lovers call it tragic . . .the end . . .curtains. Many romance stories have these themes.

Children who lose a parent often struggle with the special guilt of blaming themselves for the loss and for becoming close to a new parent figure. Adolescents grieve both the lost parent and the good years ahead that might have been, had the parent lived. This, too, is the case when a fiancé is lost or a spouse dies early in the marriage. The griever experiences the loss of a person, the special relationship, and all the fantasized stories of a new life with the loved one.

In some cases when the relationship was not going well at the time of the death or divorce, I have found the grievers to experience more grief over the happiness they did not have, the "lost years" so to speak, than at the actual loss of the person. They grieve because they feel cheated.

Grief is a healthy, though painful, reaction to loss. It is the natural and useful means whereby we find release from the attachment to persons, places, or things that have been significant to us. It is the withdrawal of ourselves from an emotional investment that has either ceased to produce positive dividends for us, or has been taken away from us. The refusal to release ourselves from someone or something that has been taken from us blocks our freedom to invest fully and joyfully in new opportunities.

Ungrieved grief, encapsulated grief, condemns a person to live in the past, emotionally and mentally. A person's history is still alive in the present. The future story is yet to be authored. Thoughts and feelings are attached to an absent person, place, or thing. The body is painfully in the present, while the spirit is tied nostalgically to the past. The past is present and the present existence is turned to the past instead of to the future.

Vision comes from the creation of more hopeful future stories. When a death has occurred, the transition from the past to the present can be made only through the "valley of the shadow of death." The refusal or inability to grieve deeply enough to release the plot of the past condemns us to a future of digging up old stories of the dead. The grieving person becomes like the dead, continuously burying the dead. Trying to proceed in life under the influence of encapsulated grief is like the driver who tries to see where he is going by looking in the rearview mirror.

Chapter Eight

Vows in Love and Loss

"The memory that an oath or vow has been made will nerve one to abstinences and efforts otherwise impossible."

William James

Whe a love ends, the stories we tell ourselves about that love can have long-lasting effects in our lives. We can revise the story to say we never really loved, or we can vow to always love that person. Love and oaths of loyalty go hand in hand, as lovers exchange their words of affection and determine to let no one come between them. "I love you and always will," or "There will never be anyone I love as much as I love you," or "I swear there will never be anyone to take your place," or "I promise to be true to you forever." These innocent and sincere words of commitment between two sweethearts or friends help to cement the bonds of a relationship. They may be the prelude to more formal declarations of loyalty such as wedding vows, when the two promise love and fidelity to one another.

Vows and oaths reach deep into our being. They create the primary plot of our lives as we intend to fulfill them at all costs. They often continue in force long after the relationship has terminated and the story should have been revised to include an ending.

Even if we push the vows from conscious remembrance they keep coming back to influence future commitments of a similar nature.

Vows to Love Forever

Mary was in her fifth year of marriage and seeking counsel about her inability to feel close to her husband. When I asked her to reflect upon her previous relationships with men, she started with her engagement. When I asked to go even further back, she reported several casual dating relationships. She spoke with great feeling about her boyfriend in her senior year of high school. She had gone away to college to please her parents, and fifteen months after she left home, the boyfriend decided not to wait for her and began dating someone else. When I asked what kind of promises they had made to each other, she said that she promised her boyfriend and herself that she would not let another boy get close to her. I suggested that she had kept her word, even with her husband.

Mary's story is yet another of ungrieved grief, which was reinforced by vows of commitment to the lost boyfriend. In her next counseling session, I helped her say goodbye to the old boyfriend and to grieve what should have been mourned when the breakup occurred. There is no way to count how many persons still hold to old vows of loyalty. They often refuse to develop another loving relationship, or they give themselves only partially to their mate. It is as if another partner lives, in ghost form, demanding loyalty. This is a form of emotional bigamy, in that a love relationship is going on with the real-life partner and also with the absent partner.

Vows to Never Love Again

Even more serious than vows to love someone always are vows that come out of disappointment and loss. These are words spoken in anger, guilt, and depression. The anger comes at the time of the loss, through death, divorce, or being "dumped." The one who suffers the loss may seek protection from further hurt with a vow against further vulnerability, such as, "I'll never love another person."

James was in his second marriage and still unhappy. He was asked to reflect back to when he started protecting himself from being hurt. He reported that when his first wife left him for another man he swore that another woman would not hurt him. When I asked him if he swore this to God, he smiled and said, "Yes, with expletives added!" I suggested that he ask God to release him from his vows.

In moments of significant loss, the choice between hurting and not hurting is not ours to make. Rather, it is only within our choice as to how far the grief will reach, in order to heal the brokenness. The refusal to grieve deeply spreads out the grief over a longer time—perhaps to our death—and amounts to covering over the loss rather than accepting it. The grief is buried, not completed, and the story has no way to end. It keeps going like a stuck record player, playing the same tune again and again, the same plot continuing to its tragic end. Guilt over a loss often encapsulates the grief story, thus keeping it from being reauthored.

Christy continued to cry two years after the death of her husband. She received plenty of sympathy and was almost addicted to people taking care of her. Her husband's insurance settlement was enough to give her a reason not to work. She became very angry at my suggestion that her life had improved since her husband's death. This re-interpretation of her story caused her to reflect upon the radical changes in her life that led her to seek counseling. She poured out her story about how unhappy she had been in the marriage, often wishing something would happen to her husband! She didn't have the courage to divorce him, but when death brought the fulfillment of her wishes, she became trapped in her guilt. The best way to disguise her guilty feelings (even to herself) was to cry. At least this provided sympathy from friends and family members. She vowed not to he happy again. She was stuck in her own sad ending of a marriage. She told only the good parts of the story of her marriage and denied the painful abusive aspects of the story. When she finally told the story of the painful experiences of her marriage and expressed her feelings of remorse and regret by writing letters to her deceased husband her crying ceased and she found relief in her grief.

Release from Vows

Vows, be they explicit promises or internal resolutions, be they spoken during the ecstasy of love or at the loss of someone we love, have a powerful and long-lasting effect upon us because they bind us spiritually to the person we vowed to always love.

Our vows shape our life stories and reinforce our commitments. They should be carefully spoken if we wish to avoid emotional damage that comes from loss and grief over losses. We have special occasions such as weddings when we make our vows, but we have no rituals or ceremonies for releasing ourselves from vows. The need for release from our vows is essential when the relationship has terminated. We cannot fully terminate the relationship as long as the vows are active.

One way to gain freedom from old vows is to request a release from the one who was the object of the vow in the first place. If it was made to another person, that one can most likely give permission to discontinue the vow. If the vow was made to God, then prayers of release should be addressed to God. If the vow was made to oneself, then permission must be granted from within.

Without warning, Steve's wife, Sue, announced that she no longer wanted to be married to him and asked that he move out of the house. Steve was in shock and disbelief at this sudden turn of events in what he thought was a happy marriage. Later he discovered that Sue was seeing another man. All of Steve's attempts to save the marriage failed, but marriage counseling did help them make decisions about parenting their children. Sue moved out of the house. With the help of the counselor, Steve grieved the loss of the marital relationship. His major conflict was over the vows of his marriage made to God, both families and friends, and especially to Sue. He saw the vows as a lifelong spiritual commitment.

A Christian friend suggested that Steve write a letter to God, asking for release from the vows once made in complete sincerity, but now impossible to keep, and take it to the altar of the church to pray for release from the vows. He also suggested that Steve ask Sue to meet with the counselor and a co-counselor, and at that time give her back his wedding ring with the request that she release him from his vows of marriage. After doing this, Steve reported that he felt much better, more reconciled to give up his marriage vows. He was still sad over the divorce but ready to move on with his life. Specific request for release from a moral commitment helped him revise the story of his divorce.

When the situation does not allow one to communicate directly, symbolic communication can be almost as effective. This can take the form of a letter detailing the history of the vow, the changes that have taken place, and the requests for release from the vow. As the grieving person destroys the letter, she can turn loose the vows made to the other person. I've found this method to be effective with persons grieving the death of a sweetheart or spouse. It also helps to complete the cycle of the story of the relationship with a living person who might cause embarrassment in their reaction to such a request.

Vows are intended to be kept at all costs, but sometimes the cost is much too high. At other times the cost is foolish, because the reason for making the vow no longer exists. All that remains is the stubborn determination to keep the vow or never to be happy again. At such a point the person must ask, "Is my life worth a vow? Can I live a new story, instead of reliving a dead one?"

Crucial Questions about Grief

Our life story is very important to us. The longer we live, the more stories we have. When we complete the stages or work of grief and successfully maneuver the transition, we acquire strength for facing the future. The biggest danger to our future is the incomplete closure of the past. In a paradoxical sense, our stories of the past are incomplete and not totally available to us until we finish the chapters that include the dead as dead, or the absent as truly absent. A major task of the counselor is to help counselees complete those chapters. Then the counselees have freedom and creativity to write new chapters. Important questions about grief include the following:

1. Do you find yourself telling yourself or others stories about the past as if something was unfinished?
2. Do you find yourself compelled to return in fact or fantasy to the past?
3. Do you hold onto hostile or hurt feelings that caused the loss?
4. Are you so full of the past experiences that you are losing the joy and creativity of the present?
5. Are you creating satisfying stories about your future?

The story of the loss may seem rather insignificant to others but major to the one who is suffering from the loss. Many experiences of losing what is significant to us, be it a cat, a car, a garden, a tree, a job, an office, the seashore, or a good fishing place may appear to be unworthy of grief. At first we may feel embarrassed to actually name the loss and let it be publicly known that we are grieving over it. We may even try to convince ourselves not to grieve anything so "silly." But we do need to grieve over what was lost, or we risk losing a more hopeful future!

Birthing and Restorying

Grief has its own built-in story line. A narrative reauthoring of the relationship story line can allow for gradual release, relief and revision of the story. The griever needs permission and assistance to pass through the painful steps of grief story. In a sense, grief is analogous to natural childbirth. The contemporary movement toward natural childbirth came from a revolt against too much or too little help, both of which can harm the baby or the mother. In recent years we have begun to return birthing to the normal life experience it was meant to be. Special help is given only in emergencies.

Life experiences of death, separation, or grief are also normal processes where informed, caring persons who know what to do or not to do are needed. What is most helpful in time of grief is the presence of supportive persons who care, who know what not to say, but who know how to ask good questions that assist the restorying process.

Retelling the story of the relationship is one important way to help a person in grief. This may be done all at once or in stages according to the time available and the energy of the griever. The support person helps the griever tell the story in a way that facilitates catharsis or flushing out of the grief.

Grief is a wound that requires mourning in order to heal. One way that healing is prevented is to let vows made to the loved one (or vows made to oneself at a time of loss) cover, block out, or otherwise encapsulate the wound. Many have found relief through restorying the life of the relationship, including the part about the loss, in the presence of a caring counselor

Not to grieve is to get stuck in ongoing denial, anger, bargaining, or depression. We have no choice about getting hurt through loss, for loss comes to all of us in life; we also have no choice about being caught up in prolonged grief. The choice we do have is whether to grieve completely so that healing will come and we will be comforted and made strong. Attempts to block, deny, hide, or ignore our grief result in perpetual hurt by the uncompleted grief. But the story does not need to end there. The past-present is important, but we fail to live in the present-present until we create a more hopeful future-present story.

Chapter Nine

Grief Stories

"Blessed are those who mourn, for they will be comforted."
Matthew 5:4

M rs. Peabody received a call telling her to come to the hospital where her husband had been admitted following an accident. She feared that it happened while he was driving under the influence of alcohol, and her fears were confirmed at the hospital. She waited long hours with her three teenagers until the surgeon and the chaplain came to tell her that her husband had died during surgery.

The chaplain stayed with them, listening to them talk about their husband-father who was also an alcoholic. The family's mixed emotions of love and anger were freely expressed along with tears. The chaplain asked Mrs. Peabody to tell him how she and her husband first met and what they liked about each other. He asked how long they dated, about their engagement, the wedding and first house, the jobs they had done and places they had lived. He carefully walked the family through their history, often stopping for waves of tears as they recalled both happy and sad times. He brought them through the most painful part of the recent history and to the point of the fatal accident. He was then able to say to them, "Now your husband, your father, is dead. It seems you have a new chapter in your family history." The chaplain helped them review their background before talking with them about important decisions that had to be made for the funeral and the future.

The chaplain was trained in crisis intervention and grief work. With this family he used the "rearview mirror" approach to grief work. This is like taking a good look in the mirror when a crisis occurs to see what is behind, before looking out of the windshield into the future. Naturally, the windshield is more important than the rearview mirror; however, both are necessary for safe driving. The memories are stored in the rearview mirror. The windshield holds the vision of a potential future. In acute grief, the past and painful present hold sway.

Looking Back

Following are some steps that pastoral counselors can use to help grieving persons review the history of a person, place, or thing irretrievably lost.

1. Be genuinely interested in the story. Find ways to assist the telling so that facts and feelings about important events are fully expressed.
2. Remain nonjudgmental. People experiencing grief feel enough guilt and judgment. Listen to their opinions about the story of the deceased and the past relationship.
3. Find an appropriate time and setting for telling the story. Some people are embarrassed or afraid to be honest in front of others listening to the history.
4. Be prepared for different versions of the story during various stages of grief. A deceased relative who was seen in an idealized light soon after the death may be viewed differently weeks later.
5. Give encouragement for the expression of feelings. Grievers may need to know it is permissible to cry in your presence. Provide tissue or handkerchief as a signal

that crying is acceptable.

6. Where the grief has been encapsulated, encourage expression of feelings and thoughts through writing a letter (not to be mailed) to the deceased. A visit to the cemetery may uncap the encapsulated grief.

7. Ask the griever to show you a series of pictures or photographs of the deceased. Seeing the pictures may facilitate the grief process, even years after the loss.

As counselors we need to know what we are doing with grief work, and why we are doing it, as we help persons allow their history to become past tense, instead of a constantly relived present tense. This is called helping the "almost dead" bury the dead so that they can live again through and beyond their grief. Then, and only then, are they free to look through the windshield and face the future with confidence as they create new, more hopeful stories.

The paradox of grief is that although it feels like a curse while we are going through it, we are blessed after having experienced it. Either we are made stronger through accepting the mourning process, or we are weakened by avoiding it. We are released from the deceased through the pain of grief, or condemned to bear the weight of the loss for the rest of our lives. No one likes to grieve; however, no one is healed from a significant loss without the purging release of the grief experience.

Jesus's paradoxical statement, "Blessed are those who mourn," needs to be seen in light of the consequences of refusing to grieve when an important loss has occurred. The blessing comes when the loss has finally been accepted and the finished grief has created space for new life stories. Such individuals are whole again and able to establish healthy relationships with others. They are a blessing to be around because their hearts are actively present in the now, instead of looking with nostalgia to the past.

Some people perceive grief as a threat, especially those afraid of strong emotions and those who have the common tendency to label emotions as good or bad. There is no mourning without the expression of emotions. The blessing proceeding from mourning is the freedom that comes after the emotions are safely and fully expressed. How these emotions are storied will depend upon individual personality dynamics and the cultural context.

A Personal Story of Grief

Grief comes in three basic forms: anticipatory, present, and encapsulated (unfinished and blocked) from the past. Grief needs to be considered in all stages of life, because it can occur over events and processes as well as over living beings such as pets or plants. Most of all, grief is experienced over the loss of loved ones. Grief is a loss, a wound, and grief wounds can be cleansed only with tears and reauthoring the relationship. The following story of a grief that was well managed, contrasts dramatically with encapsulated grief.

Jim learned that his father was diagnosed with inoperable cancer. The full impact of this information did not hit him until he made a special trip to see his father. As he left the family home, he was able to drive no more than a block before a flood of tears blinded his eyes, forcing him to pull over to the side of the street. Jim was in anticipatory grief. The system of denial surrounding him crumbled as he remembered how his father said good-bye. Jim doubted that he would ever see him alive again and began preparing himself for his father's death. Two months later his brother called to say their father would die very soon. Jim later wrote about his initial reaction:

> *I couldn't believe what my brother was saying and felt a numbness come over me. I knew my brother wouldn't have called me if Dad were not in serious condition, but I couldn't comprehend the fact that he would soon be dead. I felt confused. The fact could not register in my mind. I was dazed. As I made preparation to go home, there were no tears, only numbness.*

Shock, numbness, and denial are usually the first stage of grief in sudden, unexpected loss experiences. The mind and emotions become temporarily numbed to the pain of the loss. The most commonly heard expression is, "Oh, no!" Everything in us says no to the reality of loss.

In encapsulated grief, the mind accepts the fact of the loss, but the emotions are another story. Emotions do not approve of the reality and wage war on the mind, refusing to acknowledge the facts. Thus, the person becomes sandwiched in between reality and what used to be. These conflicting stories are fierce and quite painful. To accept a future story without human contact with the person whose life hangs in the balance forces a reauthoring of one's life story.

While flying to the family home, Jim wrote in his diary:

I love my dad. But I honestly wish he'd hurry up and die. I cannot miss too much work. Let's just get it over with. I know that I sound like a creep, but why should I lie about it? . . . .

If my dad is going to die, he'd better wait until I get home. Oh, I don't care. Let's get it over with. I hate to see him— and me—suffer. Why does it have to be this way?

Jim's emotional reactions were anger mixed with fear. He dreaded going home to face his feelings about his father's death, and he honestly portrayed his feelings about this in his diary. In encapsulated grief, however, the ambivalence is not allowed to surface to conscious awareness to become storied grief. The lost person or place is seen as being totally good or totally bad. Mixed feelings remain hidden or become split between the good and the bad feelings about the dying person.

As often happens when a person we love dies, we are forced to reexamine our relationship with God. Jim's mixed feelings about his father spilled over toward God. Thus, the loss of a significant other may be reflected in stories about loss of faith in God. The grieving person may in anger blame God for the death or in guilt blame self for not rescuing the dying person. It takes a mature, well-integrated person to accept the full range of mixed feelings.

I hate you, God! . . . .I do not want to be mad at God. I am upset with my dad for dying. God, I dread going home.

A common characteristic of persons in unresolved grief is that they have not faced the blame, anger, and guilt. Someone did something wrong and they will not be forgiven. This can be projected onto others or incorporated into oneself. Forgiveness is lacking. Resentment prevails. Jim continued his story:

When I arrived at the airport my brother-in-law met me and immediately informed me that Dad had died. I became angry. Why did he tell me so suddenly? I was mad and relieved at the same time. My heart felt ripped apart. I walked a few steps. My brother-in-law kept talking, but I could hardly hear his words. I asked if I could sit down. Then I cried body-wrenching sobs that hurt all over.

This immediate release of emotions through crying, involving every muscle in the body, is a healthy reaction to the reality of the loss. The sooner and the deeper the grief-stricken person can do this, the better will be the recovery. In encapsulated grief work, I often facilitate the release of pent-up tears that should have been expressed when the loss first occurred. As one counselee said, "I feel like I have been walking around with a bucket of tears inside!"

Withdrawal or isolation are common reactions in grief. Jim wrote:

When I arrived home, I realized immediately that, my family was definitely in a different stage of grief than I was. They were not crying but were very calm about it all. Immediately this repulsed me and I sought asylum in a bedroom where I cried. Waves of tears came. I tried to hold them back, but they kept coming.

Jim is describing the normal reaction to acceptance of death. The waves of grief offer the best, though the most painful, hope for healing. The griever's health depends upon the release of the emotions. Encapsulated grievers have been cheated from experiencing body-cleansing grief after a loss. Instead, they are condemned to a lifetime of nearly imperceptible grief that keeps the tears locked inside.

Jim's next stage could easily be predicted by persons familiar with the process of grief.

I had difficulty and confusion as I walked around the house. I listened to hear my father cough or talk. I expected to see him any minute. My memories played tricks on me. The denial of his death could no longer stand unchallenged in the face of the emptiness of the house. My mind did not give up the fantasy that he was not really dead, without a struggle.

Jim knew that his mind was playing tricks on him. He stood between life as it had been and the reality of life without the familiar presence of his father. The encapsulated griever often gets trapped in mind games. The loss is accepted factually, but the fantasy games of "if only" or "not really" still prevail. The dead one is only partially dead. The living one is only partially alive. The story is frozen in time.

When Jim saw the body of his father, he was still in a form of denial:

I looked at the flowers and at the clothes he was wearing. I thought about the socks that would keep his feet warm. I touched his face. Then the loss hit me in my gut. I knew I had to let him go. I cried and cried, and I envied the women who could cry more easily than the men. Maybe that is why they live longer. Most of the men were unable to openly express their grief.

Jim came to the moment of acceptance of the death when he encountered the lifeless body of his father. With his tears he released his father to the company of the dead. He made a radical revision in his life story that had included his father as a living person. In contrast, the encapsulated griever has not taken the decisive step of releasing the deceased. The lost person is no longer alive, but neither is he buried. The encapsulated griever sees all the details, but fails to experience the personal significance of the loss.

Jim was on his way through the normal grief process. Yet, he still had much grieving to do, though on a different level.

> *After the funeral, I was depressed and so lonely. I realized more and more that I have actually lost my father. He was such a meaningful part of my life. Why did he have to die? I will miss him. It helped me to cry when I saw the flowers and read each card; I realized how much the sympathy meant to me.*

A loss of energy and a sense of loneliness after a major loss are normal reactions for a period of three to twelve months. Short-term depression serves the purpose of conserving energies and allowing the healing process to reach into various levels of the personality. It is the long-term lack of enjoyment in life after a major loss that we call encapsulated grief. The grief has not been released. The person's story is stuck in the grief process. Time does heal the brokenhearted, except for the encapsulated griever, for whom time only prolongs the suffering because it prolongs the story of the loss. A person remains trapped in bondage to grief until release comes from an outside source.

Eighteen months after his father's death, Jim returned to his reflections:

> *The most intense period of grieving was the six months immediately following my father's death. This was a time when the tears of mourning came easily and usually very unexpectedly. There were several times that I broke down and wept almost uncontrollably months after Dad's death. Comments, memories, or certain mannerisms of people would remind me of Dad and trigger a strong emotional release. During this time of mourning I experienced a tremendous sense of loss, unlike any other I had ever experienced.*
>
> *I think the initial shock of Dad's death protected me from experiencing all this at once. But as the sense of shock*

wore off over the days and weeks, the reality of Dad's death became more apparent. It was as if God designed my mind to break the news to me gently. In many ways, the sense of shock is like romantic love. It's blinding and anesthetizing. I believe this enabled me to handle the loss a little bit at a time until I was able to handle more of the reality of death.

Jim's suffering during the normal stages of grief was mostly emotional. However, there were physiological effects as well.

I felt drained and tired most of the time. I believe this was a result of the increased emotional and mental energy needed to cope with the intensity of the grief experience. My blood pressure went from a normal 125/80 to a consistent 150/110. I've heard that elevated blood pressure is a natural anesthesia. Yet I wondered about the effect it would have on my body.

Not enough evidence has been collected to establish the precise correlation of destructive results from normal versus encapsulated grief, but the evidence seems to point in the direction of vast adverse effects, which occur over a much longer period of time for the encapsulated griever. Normal grief gradually restores us to life. Encapsulated grief may gradually lead to death.

Jim's reflection of his grief experience gives us further insight into the spiritual dimension of grief. His struggles are common to normal grief, and he was honest and open with his feelings toward God.

The acute period of grief was accompanied by intense faith struggles. My anger toward God eventually resulted in my questioning the existence of God. When Dad died, God died also. More correctly stated, my concept of God had to change if there was to be a God in my life. Dad's death destroyed my concept of the miracle-working, always intervening God. It took me months to develop a concept of God as caring and present, not always handing out miracles, but a God who allowed death. I have a new understanding of God's grace. I didn't have to like Him or even believe in Him for Him to love me. I discovered that He loved me even when I was angry with Him. He believed in me even when I did not believe in Him.

Sufferers in encapsulated grief may hold a grudge story against God for robbing them of the life that once existed. Some grieving persons try to appease God for all the hateful thoughts they had during the intense suffering. Many devout religious persons live in intense fear of a vengeful God who will get back at them for their anger. Others may become more religious to overcome their negative ambivalence toward the deceased. Death frees them from bondage to the deceased, but they take on a new bondage called guilt. They are glad the dead person is dead, but they feel guilty for feeling that way.

Jim finished his reflection about the positive effects of the grief experience:

My grief experience has been a catalyst for personal growth in almost every area of my life. I feel much more aware of my own feelings and I am definitely more sympathetic to others who suffer great losses. I feel like my personality and outlook have gone through positive changes since my dad's death. The grief process is not completely over. Christmas was very hard and quite sad. I still miss Dad and think of him often. The loss was real. With healing has come hope. Yet, I am still growing through the experience and receiving the help of others who care. But even now I feel better about myself and my future.

The major difference between healthy and encapsulated grief is that the first produces growth through suffering. Healthy grief releases the emotions and chemical toxins associated with grief. Storying the grief allows room for restorying the relationship.

Encapsulated grief is incomplete grief, like an unfinished story, thereby preventing growth and the healing processes. With unfinished grief, the blessing from mourning is yet to be received, because the grief continues in the hidden recesses of the griever's life. The bondage of ungrieved grief is the curse of living with the dead. The plot of the story becomes an unending repetition of living in the past.

Jim's story helps us understand the normal stages of grief. Blessings from mourning await those who fully grieve their losses. Verbal and affective expressions of grief bring the past present of the relationship into the present-present. When grieving is well done, the future as seen from the present shows hope like that expressed by Jim:

But even now I feel better about myself and my future.

Children and Loss

Before they reach the teenage years, children suffer many losses because they have so little control over their world. They must move geographically when their family moves; they cannot stop their parents from divorcing. Their pets die or run away. They can be separated from their friends by teachers, principals or by the friends' families that move away. Their losses are both large and small, but to a small child, all losses are big because their sense of place changes, and the plot of their story makes a radical shift.

The most profound loss to small children is the death of a parent, brother, or sister. The first thing to bear in mind about helping children with this kind of loss is that they might sometime have wished the loved one dead and created fantasy stories about life without them. Because children have only a relatively simple and unsophisticated sense of cause and effect, they very often assume that their wish was the cause of the death and are terrified to tell anyone about it.

With all children who have lost a loved one, it is important that a caring adult speak with them several times at length about what has happened and what the children are feeling and thinking, especially in the stories they may have created about the deceased. If the children have developed a story of personal responsibility, this gives opportunity to set things straight.

In this same vein, children need reassurance about any other guilt and regrets they might be experiencing about the loved one's time with them on earth. Regrets about not being a better boy or girl, not being more helpful, not visiting the loved one more, not taking better care of the loved one during illness, and forgetting a birthday are just a few of the concerns they might be struggling with.

Younger children may have misconceptions about what death means. Each of these misconceptions, usually in the form of self-stories, needs to be talked through in a reassuring manner. Some of the more common misconceptions include the idea that dead people are only sleeping and will be buried alive. Perhaps they will wake up underground and starve to death or suffocate, or may be left all alone, forever locked in the coffin. Another misconception is that the mortician will kill them.

Children often believe that their loved ones will get lonely for them in heaven. Sometimes they wonder if there will be anything to eat in heaven, or if there will be a Christmas tree or birthday parties or friends. Children often think that God "did this" to the loved one and might get the child next. They may also wonder whether the loved one can still hear them.

The younger the child, the more important it is to reassure and also to challenge false assumptions in concrete language. For example, the small child who asks if Grandpa will have a rocking chair in heaven could be assured that Grandpa will have whatever he needs to be happy in heaven. Children create their own stories from bits and pieces of information from adults and their imaginations.

Helping children grieve means to cry with them, to share emotional reactions with them, to tell stories and to let them know that adults, too, are sad, depressed, hurt, and bewildered. Children also need to know of our faith in life after death. They need to learn of our hope—that we grieve, but not as those who have no hope. Those who believe in life after death must realize that both believers and nonbelievers grieve, for it is human to grieve at loss. The difference is that Christian believers grieve a loss to themselves, knowing that the lost one lives on in eternity.

Children, like adults, are suffering losses all the time. They lose friends, teachers, their school, their homeroom teacher, pets, homes, bedrooms, toys. These events can become opportunities for helping children learn to grieve and heal from loss. When these losses can be prevented, it is good to do so. For example, if the next promotion means a move, the needs of the children should be considered in making the decision. If a move is to be made, parents should be sure to help their children prepare for the inevitable losses.

A mother asked me to talk with her teenage daughter whose cat had been killed. The girl felt that she had lost a close friend, and yet she couldn't explain her grief to people for fear of ridicule. She was surprised to learn that such love and such grief did not mean she was sick or crazy. She had invested a good part of herself in this cat. When it died, a part of herself was torn away. I asked her to bring pictures of her cat to our next session. She brought a full album of pictures, many of which were taken with her own camera. Our time together was spent in relating the joys and heartaches of loving and losing a pet. As she wept over the death of her cat and told me stories about it, her depression lifted.

Children, just as much as adults, invest themselves in what they love. Although their losses may be devastating, the scale of their world is often too small for adults to notice. For example, the loss of a little friend may seem insignificant to the adults of the family, when they notice that their child has many other friends who all seem to be alike. A child may be crying herself to sleep, while the parents are discussing in another room "how well" she is doing! It is crucial to take the grief of children seriously, all of it! Help them tell their stories, no matter how unbelievable they may be.

Other Losses

As adults we suffer a great many losses other than death. Perhaps the most frequent of these happens during and after a divorce. Here the loved one is definitely lost, and in addition, there is the blow of rejection which comes from being abandoned by one who is still alive and who may choose another lover. Divorce is traumatic for the same reasons that death of a loved one is traumatic.

Our self-stories were invested in the loved one, and now these stories and emotional attachments are ripped out, and the wound bleeds with hurt and grief.

What is lost in divorce is not only a loved one but a way of life, a love story, a set of assumptions about life, the marriage relationship along with the friends and relatives attached to it. Such a loss is usually accompanied by a drop in self-confidence and self-esteem (no one else likes me and neither do I), followed by feelings of failure. We also get angry, feel hurt, depressed, isolated, afraid, and insecure. Letting the story of the relationship become history takes a methodic, organized effort that needs to be scheduled if it is going to happen. The tears, the questions, telling the story of the relationship, both good points as well as negative ones, praying—all this and more needs to be done.

In addition to divorce are other major kinds of loss, such as destruction of a home in a storm, loss of a job, bankruptcy (loss of credit and self-esteem). Just like death and divorce, these losses represent serious upheaval and personal devastation. They are to be dealt with by grieving over a period of time, until they become integrated into our history, and we become free of the rancor, depression, and constant looking to the past.

Grieve to Heal

The first thing we need to remember about grieving losses is that grief is a process: the deeper the loss, the deeper the wound, and the longer it takes to heal. In the case of a close loved one, the healing process takes six months to a year or even two years. That does not mean, of course, months and years of nonstop crying and anger; but, reauthoring the relationship takes time. Restorying the history of the relationship with a narrative oriented counselor can significantly shorten the time and the suffering of the grieving person. Jesus said: "Blessed are they who mourn." The blessing is bestowed upon the mourner from the redemptive process of story-telling and story-listening.

The purpose of grief is to heal. Blessed are those who mourn . . .

not because grieving is fun, and not because sorrow really isn't sorrow. Blessed are those who mourn a loss, compared with those who will not grieve their losses. Those who are willing to mourn shall be healed of their losses. To be healed of grief is to become whole and strong enough again, to go on living fully with the memory of the lost loved one or thing, but without all the grieving emotions of that loss, once the grief is completed and the loss has become history. To mourn is to cheat death of any more than what death has already claimed. It is to let the dead be dead, but allow the living to live fully, free from the shadow of death. It is not to die before our time. It is to accept our stories of the past-present, present-present and future-present. Then we are healed of our losses and open to new love and new life, to the creation of new chapters in our life story with the presence of important supporting characters who influenced us in the past.

Chapter Ten

Faith Conversations

"To follow a story is to actualize it by hearing it."

Paul Ricour

Jennifer and Paul's disagreements about church spilled over into other areas of their marriage. Jennifer grew up in an evangelical family where her faith developed after a personal commitment to Jesus Christ and regular attendance at various church activities. She took her faith seriously. While they were dating, Mike attended worship services with her and was supportive of her spiritual commitments. But shortly after the wedding, he reverted back to his family's practice of attending church on special occasions such as Christmas Eve and Easter. At first she tried to understand his desire to stay home to rest from his busy week at work and went to church by herself. But she missed the emotional and spiritual satisfaction she felt when they were in church together. Some Sundays she found herself envying other couples who worshiped together. The well-meaning questions of friends about her husband's absence only increased the lack of spiritual intimacy with her husband.

Pleading with Paul to attend church with her led to arguing and arguing led to occasional withdrawal of physical affection, especially on weekends. He interpreted their diminishing intimacy as something physically wrong with her. His personal satisfaction shifted to his work, which in turn led to fatigue and further distancing from his wife. Their marriage was on a downward spiral.

A major blowup of yelling and crying shocked them into realizing they needed help. Paul reluctantly agreed to go with Jennifer to talk with a pastoral counselor.

During our first conversation, they shared their struggles over church attendance and a lack of intimacy. Each had a different version of the story. Following my request that they choose a name to identify the central issue, they made several suggestions, some of which were about each other, but eventually agreed on the word "church." I quickly admitted that as a pastoral counselor I could not be neutral on the issue, but could help them talk about the role of faith in their marriage and how it might be expressed through attending church. I was fully aware that religious differences could produce difficulties in other areas of their marriage. However, I did not want to shift the attention to psychological, or physical issues in their intimacy, a tendency of many counselors who feel uncomfortable with spiritual assessments.

Couples often struggle with both spiritual and physical intimacy. I picture this as an acrostic, S-I-S. The I stands for intimacy. One S represents spirituality, the other sexuality. Sexuality and spirituality are dynamically connected to one's history, feelings, and experiences with intimacy. Some people use jokes and curse words in an attempt to dispel anxiety related to both sexuality and spirituality. One reason for the Christian value placed on clean language is to recognize intimacy as part of God's good creation. But, clean language itself does not necessarily mean a person is comfortable with intimacy.

I inquired about Jennifer's and Paul's spiritual faith journeys. As each one told me their religious background and faith stories, the other discovered aspects of each other they had never known before. My primary purpose was not to look for information in order to help them with their problems; rather, I wanted to help them restory their relationship as they responded to the questions. My not-knowing-but-wanting-to-learn attitude enabled them to genuinely hear about each other's faith experiences. Both telling and listening to a story creates a new version of the story, thereby changing the individuals' understanding of it. My role in the reauthoring dialogue was to provide a forum for putting into their own words the thoughts and feelings they had not been able to share with each other.

My trust in the presence of the Holy Spirit as the Third Person in the conversation, and my belief in a narrative process, helped them respect their differences so they could start to work toward things they could agree upon. Telling their story with the help of my questions made each one an authority on the subject of his and her own faith journey I wanted my concern for each spouse as a unique and special person to help demonstrate God's concern for their individuality and their relationship.

Once we heard Jennifer's and Paul's personal faith stories, I shifted my questions to the stories they had each been telling themselves about the other. This moved us into more dangerous waters, since most of us get upset when someone tells a different version of the story than we tell ourselves. I think of these as pre-understandings waiting for verification or revision. Conversations create new understandings of a subject matter, not only for the counselor but also for others engaged in the conversation. I find this part of the conversation to be one of the most helpful to couples. It seems to clear up misconceptions so they can communicate better with each other.

In their differences about attending church, this couple had lost the grace to respectfully listen to each other about their personal beliefs and practices. Their differences blinded them to what attracted them to each other in the first place. Unfortunately, religion had become a point of contention rather than a means for achieving greater intimacy with God and with each other.

Reauthoring the Faith Story

The following questions are examples of the ones I use when talking with couples about their faith issues. I ask some or all of them according to the flow of the conversation. In this account I use J for Jennifer and P for Paul.

1. J or P. "I know a little about your background, but I don't know much about your religious upbringing. Could you give me some idea of what that was like for you? (Explore the details with other questions.)
2. When the story seems completed, ask the other partner, "What did you hear that was new or different?" And, "What was it like for you to hear this story today?"
3. Ask each spouse, "Before you married, how much did you know about the spiritual life of your spouse? Was this important to you then? How have you changed during the marriage? What do you tell yourselves about these changes? How have you let your spouse know about these changes?"
4. Find the points where the spiritual life of each spouse is not a problem in their relationship. "What happens when you do not allow this problem to influence your happiness with each other?" Explore this to find out when they are able to cooperate with each other without compromising their beliefs.
5. Help them develop a vision of what life without the problems will be like. "How will you know when this issue is no longer a concern for you? As you resolve this issue in your relationship, how will you describe your achievement a year from now? How would you picture your relationship when you resolve this issue and _____ is no longer disturbing your marriage?"
6. Ask, "Who would you most likely talk with about your spiritual concerns?"
7. Ask, "Have you been praying about this concern? Have your prayers been answered?"
8. Help them find both wisdom and strength from God to draw them out of their predicament. Ask, "How should I pray for you about this part of your marriage? How will you know and be able to share with me that the prayers are being answered?"

I usually give an achievable assignment before our next

conversation. I might ask them to observe the times when the problem does not interfere with their marriage. I suggest they look for small signs that the other partner is supporting, rather than pushing or pulling against, the other's spiritual journey.

Faith Counseling Is Not Value-Free

No counselor is neutral about faith issues, but most try to be impartial in counseling conversations. All statements and questions carry assumptions and presuppositions about what is acceptable and important to participants in the conversation. This means that all conversations include certain values.

I believe that a narrative approach to faith counseling helps to achieve fairness in the conversation, especially with spouses. As they each have a turn to tell a story, they should be able to see that the counselor is not actively supporting the position of one over the other.

Each partner has their own religious perspective that either helps or hinders them in resolving their problems. My perspective will be expressed in some form—they expect me to have Christian values and practices and would be disappointed in my pastoral leadership if I did nothing more than listen to them. They already have some idea about what I believe.

Narrative pastoral counselors use the competencies of counselees to help them resolve their problems. This demands discipline from the counselor, because it is much easier to point out problem areas and give advice than it is to create new, life-changing stories. I can best strengthen a marriage relationship when I encourage the couple to do most of the thinking and creation of their own solutions. Conversely, I weaken them when they see me as the "answer pastor." If, by chance, they create something I cannot support, I'm always free to tell them. A pastoral conversation becomes a changed story, not by what information they receive, but by help in reauthoring their story.

Paul and Jennifer brought to counseling only one theme of many themes from the story of their marriage. I saw myself as a co-author in this chapter of the story of their marriage as I helped them reauthor their faith stories. The time I conversed with them was but a small slice of the total history of their relationship. I wanted to make a difference in their relationship with God and with each other as they conversed with me. Their story was being modified through dialogue in the presence of the Holy Spirit. I did not work alone.

I saw myself as their spiritual friend, as well as someone concerned about the problems created by different approaches to the expression of their Christian faith. The more I was fully present to hear their story, the more I could enable them in the expanded exploration of their spiritual life. Helping them articulate their story in the context of their faith, including their differences, created a deeper bond of intimacy. In a real sense I was helping them create a revised and more acceptable expression of their faith. I was with them as a fellow pilgrim on a journey.

As counselees travel through their stories, I try to enjoy the scenery. I find it much easier to assist people in their spiritual lives when I ask questions that help them create future scenarios as I ask them to imagine how they want things to be with the help of God. I believe people change when they see a vision of what they would like to have happen.

Because people need a vision to aim for, much more than they need to know the cause of their problems, I try to focus on the future of their relationship. I want to talk about where they are going more than to listen to where they have been. The past plays tricks on the narrator of a story. The past is like a foreign country with its different customs and language. The future is like fresh-baked bread, full of possibilities.

Once Paul heard Jennifer's future hope of an intimate spiritual and physical relationship, he understood and accepted her desire for his participation in worship services and other church activities. This led to his own confession of faith and willingness to develop his own faith through participation in a Bible study group and a volunteer service ministry.

What if One Partner Is Disinterested?

Trouble can develop when one partner has little or no interest in a faith journey, while the other sees the integration of faith into the marital relationship as an important issue. Because rational approaches to the polarized spiritual positions seldom resolve the issues, a narrative approach proves more effective in moving the couple beyond the impasse.

Eric and Kirsten were both successful in their careers. After years of failure to conceive a child, they decided to invest in an expensive house, new cars, travel, and building their careers. Kirsten did continue to take hormones to increase the possibility of having a baby, and she became pregnant soon after they had made some major investments in their materialistic lifestyle.

Eight months into the pregnancy, doctors removed a malignant breast tumor. And, two years later, when she was diagnosed with liver cancer, their lives were thrown into complete turmoil.

A concerned neighbor referred Kirsten and Eric to me for counseling. Eric was reluctant to go to a Christian for counseling because he did not want to have anything to do with God. Kirsten had grown up in a Charismatic Christian home, but had traded this in for a religion of materialism after her marriage to a nonbeliever. Now that her life was threatened, she recalled the prayers for healing that were part of her heritage. She wanted a counselor who could relate to her spiritual needs and help with the stress and communication problems in the marriage.

When they came to me the first time, Eric said, "I want you to know that I don't want any of this Religion stuff. I don't believe in it."

I asked, "What is your religion and just how religious are you?" His response was, "What do you mean? I don't have a religion."

I asked, "Well, what are you most interested in? What do you give your passion to?"

He responded, "My career."

My answer to him was, "Then your career is your religion. That which we dedicate our lives to achieving is our religious pursuit." Then I asked if he had always been a secular religious person, he told me a story about growing up in a Texas town where his father was a very successful roofer. Their family lived in one of the best houses in the city and Eric's childhood was enjoyable. His family went to church every Sunday until he was sixteen, when a severe hailstorm destroyed every roof in town. Because of the demand, roofers came from every direction to repair the homes, and even his father's employees left to go into the private roofing business, to make money as fast as they could.

Eric watched his father go from being a respected businessman to having to declare bankruptcy, since every house in town now had a new roof. Their home had to be sold, and his father had to start over at age fifty-five at a low-paying job. Eric told me he never returned to church after that. The explanation of the hailstorm was: "an act of God."

After I responded to his story with empathy, especially to his struggle to believe in a God who would hurt his family, Eric fought back tears as he asked, "If there is a God, why did He allow this thing to happen to my family?"

Instead of answering his question, I sat in silence as he wept for the first time over the tragic circumstances his family had experienced. Then I talked with him about the vows he had made as a response to suffering.

Between trips to cancer treatment centers, I met with Eric and Kirsten spending many hours talking and praying with them. As Kirsten became more ill, I worked with the theological struggles felt by her extended family, particularly her mother and sister's "Name it and claim it" faith. As the cancer spread and Kirsten was approaching death, her mother and sister continued to pray for healing.

The day before Kirsten's death, I put my arm around her mother and my other hand on the large Bible she was using to practically demand that God heal her daughter. I gently said to her, "Mamma, it must be very hard for you to see Kirsten dying like this, and God not responding to His own word as you have begged Him to do." She broke down and wept for the first time, as I held her shaking body.

And Eric? During the months of Kirsten's illness, his faith deepened in the face of adversity. He and Kirsten received many acts of kindness from members of our church and his story about God was revised, even as they approached her death. While Kirsten was still able to attend church, they together made their public profession of faith.

Chapter Eleven

Writing Narrative Letters to Counselees

"Letters have a power of speech which tongues
do not possess."

Rabindranath Tagore

One of the most powerful ways to increase the effectiveness of the narrative conversation is to write letters, or short notes, to counselees after a meeting. I wish I had discovered this many years earlier. Even though writing them takes extra time, these letters are great time-savers.

The counseling process moves to a new level of awareness when the phrases, quotations, and references to parts of the conversation are included in a letter. A more meaningful story unfolds for me and for the counselee as the story shifts from an oral to a written narrative.

One woman reported that she kept the letter with her as a reminder of the changes she was experiencing and to give her courage to keep going. To her, it was like a mirror reflecting the changes taking place in the story of her life and the way she approached personal relationships. She saw it as much more than a summary of our previous conversation and treated it as an emotional and spiritual document of her life at that point.

The story creation that took place in conversational form continues with even greater force in a follow-up letter. The reader is able to concentrate on the meaning of the written words, when the expectation of verbal questions and conversational give-and-take are not an expected part of the communication. As I write the letter, I have more time to reflect on the conversation and include thoughts that I wish had been expressed then. A counselee reading the letter in the privacy of his or her home has more time to reflect on both the content and meaning of our conversation.

Writing narrative letters to counselees has given me a new appreciation for the letters in the New Testament. Yes, they contain much information, but the primary value of reading them is the spiritual formation of the reader. These letters continue to have a profound formative impact upon my own spiritual life, as I look at it from the perspective of the writers. I sometimes wonder how Timothy felt when he received letters from the Apostle Paul. "I, Paul, am an apostle on special assignment for Christ, our living hope. Under God our Savior's command, I am writing this to you, Timothy, my son in the faith. All the best from our God and Christ be yours!" (I Timothy 1:1-2, *The Message*) Evidently, this letter and others were worth keeping and considered worthy to be included in the canon of the Bible.

When I write a letter after a pastoral conversation, I carefully piece together the salient parts of the story's central issues. Then I give emphasis to the positive action to be taken, since the future is my primary concern. Though the future does not yet exist, it is the only part of the story that has a chance for change. The past cannot be altered, but the perspective of the past can be revised. I can explore alternative endings of the problem in the narrative letter.

As I write I frequently refer to the issue by the name the counselee has chosen to call the problem. In the conversation, we have externalized the problem by helping the counselee to name it. In the letter I refer to the counselee in the first person and the problem in the third person. This helps us create a strong alliance against the problem. In the unfolding drama of the counselee's life, the problem is consistently referred to as the antagonist and the counselee as the protagonist. Many alternative stories can be created to replace the one problematic story. The counselee gains the advantage of choosing, within certain limits, a different path than the dead-end previously taken.

Structure of the Letter

When I write narrative letters to counselees, I usually start with an introductory paragraph that reconnects the reader to our previous conversation. Then I describe some of the action of the problem story and how this has influenced the person's life. I document some of the exceptions to the power of the problem that we talked about in the counseling session, and the successful actions already taken against the problem. I include the possible decisions the counselee has considered taking against the problem. Sometimes I add thoughts and questions that came to me after the session.

To keep the reader of the letter from writing back to me, I ask that any reflections from reading the letter be shared with me in the next session. I'm careful about the information included in the letter—I don't want damaging confidential information to be read by a third party to the counseling relationship, without permission of the counselee.

Occasionally, I ask counselees to write letters to significant persons in their lives to help them find closure with a person or particular problem in the relationship. More often than not, these letters are not mailed; however, writing them creates new meaning that helps to change the relationship with the problem.

Conflict Avoidance

The following letter to a young pastor and his wife will give some ideas about the salient parts of a narrative pastoral letter.

Dear Jon and Kellie,

Most of the time counselors see couples that have so much conflict in their lives that they can no longer tolerate the stress between them. You came to see me because you discovered that you had been avoiding conflict in order to keep peace in the home. However, you now realize how much of your time, thought, and energy have been wasted with this old style of coping with conflict. You discovered you were either avoiding each other or focusing your life together on work and the needs of your children. I think you are wise to reexamine your style of coping with conflict and to seek counseling, especially at this time of transition from seminary to full time ministry.

You agreed to name the problem you are facing "Conflict Avoidance". You gave a vivid description of how it has dominated your relationship. Though you love each other very much, you were losing touch with each other as you settled for what appeared to be peace between you. You no longer felt some of the intimacy that characterized your relationship in the earlier years. Instead of avoiding the issue, you decided to do something about it before it controls your marriage.

From taking a look back to the stories of your families of origin, you have a clearer sense of how your Conflict Avoidance was created, in response to observing how your parents managed conflict. Kellie, you said you developed your model from the way your mother related to your father before they divorced when you were eleven. Jon, you saw too much conflict in your parents' marriage and made a personal vow not to have this kind of conflict when you got married. From this background you had the perfect ingredients to make a Conflict Avoidance marital relationship.

I like the way you reauthored the story of your relationship while we were talking together. This was a very tender moment for all of us. I think you started to make the transition from protecting each other to protecting your relationship. To continue your fight against Conflict Avoidance, I suggest you continue doing some of the things you have discovered work best for you, such as weekly meetings for talking, and waiting for the appropriate times to discuss your possible conflict issues. You would benefit from adding the other thing you think will be helpful to you in dealing with conflict—learning to speak directly and honestly with each other, even when it is about an unpleasant subject. I will be interested in hearing in our next session how you are doing this.

I also like the picture you described to me about your future when Conflict Avoidance is no longer controlling your relationship. You see yourselves spending less time mentally rehashing unpleasant problems, enjoying more freedom to change, and sharing more laughter and joy with each other. Kellie, you told how this would free Jon to do ministry without worrying about you being upset with him. You would balance time with each other as well as have time for the children. I especially like the idea of developing a healthier model of marriage for your children to observe.

When I asked you how Conflict Avoidance would try to sneak back into the house like an insect, you said it could happen by allowing yourselves to shift back into trying to protect each other from negative feelings, or slipping into a lack of discipline in your relationship.

I think some major changes are taking place in your relationship. You will have to keep working on these. When positive changes begin, old habits seem to fight even harder to maintain control. I pray that God will give you the discernment and the courage to keep moving in the direction you are heading, toward a more fulfilling marital relationship. I look forward to hearing how you take control of Conflict Avoidance instead of allowing it to control you. I would not be surprised to see it pack up and leave your home before very long.

Blessings in your new marriage,

Burrell

Writing this letter required an additional thirty minutes of my time. I think it saved several hours of counseling time later. At their next visit Jon and Kellie reported several satisfactory changes they had made in the interval between the sessions, including speaking more frankly to each other and being considerate about finding appropriate times to talk about their relationship. They were more concerned about caring for the relationship than protecting each other's feelings. They reported being more relaxed around each other and experiencing a new freedom in intimacy.

Fear of Rejection

A young husband asked to talk with me after an argument with his wife. He was concerned about the intensity of his emotional responses to her. His story included deep feelings of anger that were causing him to say hurtful things to her that he later regretted. Then he related a story about a former fiancee who dropped him for another man. He was remorseful for some of the things he had said to her, but had never asked her for forgiveness.

As stories develop in conversation, they often lead to more significant stories. With tears in his eyes he told of the rejection he felt from his father and the way he rebelled against him. Soon after our meeting I wrote him the following letter.

Dear Tony,

It was good to see you today and to hear about the emotional and spiritual progress you are making with your journaling. It was clear that you have determined to no longer allow the story of your past to control the way you see yourself and the way you treat people. You have decided to examine your automatic style of responding to people you feel close to, so that you can be in charge of more appropriate ways of relating. This demonstrates an intellectual and emotional growth that is starting to produce a more satisfactory lifestyle.

When I asked about your primary concern, you said it was Fear of Rejection. As I reflect upon our session, I am convinced that Fear of Rejection will have trouble ruining your life, because God is answering your prayers for knowledge of self, the ability to see yourself as lovable, and the discernment to understand that not everyone is out to get you. It was inspiring to see these prayers start to be answered as you envisioned a future that included the answer to your prayers. You felt energy and excitement in your whole body as you told me about the ways you will be living your life in relationship with other people. The answer to these prayers will help you express deep feelings that have been kept locked up inside of you.

You envisioned your preaching going through a change in response to the answer to these prayers, because you will no longer be talking just to please others. You saw each day as an exciting adventure, instead of dreaded confrontations that would reinforce Fear of Rejection. You expressed that even your friends would celebrate your release from this fear. Also, you were aware that some people would have difficulty accepting your freedom from Fear of Rejection; however, you did not seem to be too concerned about this, because the advantages would outweigh the disadvantages.

I remember you wanted to write letters to people you felt close to in the past, to express your feelings about your relationship with them. I suggest you concentrate on crafting a letter to your deceased biological father and to your former girlfriend. Even in his death your father seems to have maintained control over how you perceive yourself. In the letter you might tell him how you experienced his parenting. If you are ready, tell him that you want to ask God to forgive him and for God to give you the strength to do the same. Tell him what you plan to do with this Fear of Rejection that you have carefully guarded since you were thirteen. Since this letter cannot be mailed, why don't you bring it to your next counseling session and read it to me. Then we can decide what should be done with it.

I was pleased, but not surprised, to hear from you that other Christian friends are praying for your personal healing and the healing of your marriage. Be assured that I am doing the same.

Burrell Dinkins.

At our next appointment Tony read a very emotional letter to his father in which he poured out his love for his father and asked for forgiveness. He said this was the first time he had grieved the death of his father. A significant reauthoring of his father-son story was created through writing this letter.

At the end of our conversation he said he had called his former fiancee's brother to get her new address so he could write a letter of apology to her. He was surprised when she answered the phone. She was house-sitting while her brother was on vacation. He apologized for his past behavior, asked forgiveness, and forgave her for suddenly dropping him for the other boyfriend. They affirmed the good times they had together and said they released each other from the vows to always love each other. She wished him well in his marriage. Tony reported that a ton of weight was lifted off his shoulders after this conversation. By the creation of a new ending to his story of his old girlfriend he also created a new future for himself.

Control, Manipulation, and the Fear of Intimacy

A couple came to talk with me about changes taking place in their relationship after their children grew up and left home. They were alone for the first time since their second year of marriage and were having trouble accepting this new way of living. They wanted a better relationship, but were unable to agree on who should do the changing. After our conversation I wrote the following letter to them.

Dear Chris and Cathy,

It was good to see you last Wednesday. I was impressed with how you care for each other and how much you have helped each other achieve success in life. From our conversation it was evident to me that you are in a process of transition in your marital relationship. Both of you have matured from the time you first met. During the stage of marriage that is ending, you dedicated your passion to helping the other change, but without much progress. It could be that your commitment to helping the other one change is not needed or wanted by either of you. You might better direct your passion in another direction, mainly to find what Cathy called "Personal Contentment".

You seem to be ready to create this new love story to guide your journey into the future. The children do not need the attention they used to, and so you are freer to focus on what makes each one of you happy. Then you will be able to love each other out of the overflow of your own cup rather than filling each other's cup in hope that something might spill on yourself. Since you are the generation of your extended family that is breaking the unhappy patterns of the past, you might as well go all the way by creating new ways of loving. This has already started, even before you came for counseling.

From what Cathy said, she has learned to do a lot of things very well. She figured out how to solve a problem with the computer at work that even the computer expert could not solve. She stood up to her boss at work over his unrealistic expectation of her working on Saturday. Also, she is insisting that the children take more responsibility for themselves. Now she is standing up for herself in relationship to you, Chris. She has the belief that marriage can be more enjoyable, so she is not willing to continue to see herself trying to earn your love. She wants to develop a new way of sharing herself with you. The thing that was amazing to me is that you seemed to be very excited about the changes you see taking place in her. You said you have changed a great deal in the past year and a half. Maybe you are as ready as she is for writing a new and more enjoyable chapter in the story of your life together.

Cathy called the primary problem Control and Manipulation. Chris called it Fear of Intimacy. As I said, these seem to be closely related. I still am not sure how the two of you got recruited into this kind of relationship, but I look forward to next week to see how well you have been able to trick Control, Manipulation, and the Fear of Intimacy from managing your marriage. I will be interested to hear what you have found that helps you overcome, at least temporarily, the enemies that keep you apart.

Until Wednesday,

Burrell

At our next session, using the analogy of a video tape, I suggested that they rewind to the years when they were dating, engaged, and the first eighteen months of the marriage, and then tell me what I would see on the tape. I asked them to give me a vivid description of the early phase of their marriage when they had an enjoyable relationship.

After they told me about the early years of their marriage, I remarked," Children are like visitors; some stay longer than others, but they all eventually leave. Think of them as long-term visitors who decided that it was time to leave. Now that you have the house to yourselves, can you fast-forward the video to the present? You are free to create new scenes of your life together. Now fast-forward the story of your life together and describe for me what you would like the next chapter in your story to look like." This led to an imaginary narrative creation as they described future scenes of a couple doing things together that evidenced a happy relationship.

My next letter to them included a description of the scenes they created of a satisfactory future relationship. Creating a story and telling it is one thing. Seeing it in writing is an even stronger statement. Living out the story has yet to be done; however, a new story has to be imagined as being possible before the doing. We live the stories we tell ourselves.

Letters Highlight Conversations

As Paul Ricoeur wrote, "To follow a story is to actualize it by hearing it."[34] Hearing oneself create a story creates the conditions for actualizing it. Seeing the story in written form brings the story alive into the present moment. The time space between a narrative conversation, reading the letter, and our next appointment is as full of possibilities for restorying the counselee as the conversation itself. A changed story predates a changed life or relationship.

Narrative letters greatly contribute to the co-authoring process. When writing them I want to give a faithful summary of the co-authored story from our conversation. Then I give my opinions of the conversation's effect on the counselee and on me. Before concluding the letter I offer suggestions for continuing the storying process, assuming the narrative process will accelerate after the letter is read. The letters are meant to piece together in words what the counselee has always known but has suppressed in favor of alternative stories, to facilitate in the expression of pent-up emotions, and to point toward a more hopeful future. To read that a person is a survivor instead of a victim has a powerful impact upon the reader. In other words, the letters create meaning and experiences, and lead to the creation of new stories.

The letters are written in the present tense, about the past-present conversation, but the future as seen from the present. The restorying of the future of the counselee's narrative is the primary concern. As the counselee reads the print of the letter with the quotes, phrases, and summary of our dialogue, his own words take on new meaning. The act of reading often creates new motivation for reauthoring the script. The letter can trigger openings in the story that were previously unseen.

I use letters to highlight key parts of the narrative conversation that need revision or affirmation and to help open space for reauthoring troublesome parts of the narrative of the counselee. The letters are but one event in the narrative conversations, but a very important one. They are more than an appendage to the narrative conversation.

White and Epston believe that the letters are a substantially new way of understanding narrativity in a counseling relationship. Letters are more than physical documents. They are psychological and have deep emotional potential for change in counselees. The letters are written primarily for the purpose of rendering lived experiences into a story that makes sense to the writer and the reader according to the structure of narrative coherence.[35] The letters can affirm change and generate more hopeful stories. A future worth living has to be imagined as story worth believing before it is realized.

Chapter Twelve

Confidentiality:
The Hidden Minefield

"Use your public role as a performer to conceal from others, and
possibly from yourself, what is going on in private."
Roger C. Schank

Counseling can be dangerous to your integrity. Handle with
care. Sharing stories increases your concern for another
person and also the possibility that this concern may lead to liking,
and liking to loving, and that loving could end in inappropriate
touching, and touching to sexual intimacy. Privacy and confidentiality of conversation increases the risk of boundary violations.

A seminary student wrote the following letter to me about a
valuable lesson he learned while visiting with his parents.

*"I frequently mention to people the lessons I learn from
other people's mistakes. Simply seeing how a person's life
can be completely ruined or altered by some bad choices
helps me reflect on how I can avoid the same mistakes.
During spring reading week, my father and I headed off on
a backpacking trip. We had trouble finding the trail due to*

some unexpected construction. A dead-end dirt road took us up the mountain we knew the trail was on and we thought it might lead us to the trail. On the way, we saw a couple in a car in this remote place. When we first drove past, we realized that the couple was behaving in a very intimate manner.

"When we failed to find the trail at the end of the road, we turned around and approached the car on our way down the mountain. The couple was trying to push the car back on the road so we stopped to offer some assistance. My father recognized the man as a well-known pastor of a church in our area, but the woman was not his wife. My father is a superintendent in the same denomination as this pastor.

"After prayer and reflection, my father reported what we saw to the man's superintendent. When confronted with the accusation, the pastor admitted the woman was not his wife, but denied that he was doing anything wrong. He was not repentant for his behavior. He was given the option either to continue denying the charges, which would call for a full investigation, or to announce his retirement the following Sunday. Without hesitation he chose the second option.

"This event was a lesson to me because of the pastor's reputation. He was frequently held up as a great Christian counselor and often had cases referred to him from other pastors. My father is a pastoral counselor, which made reporting the incident even more painful to him.

"The lesson I got out of this is the importance of integrity. I believe my father acted responsibly by reporting the incident. The integrity of each individual pastor directly affects his or her ministry. I have heard people lament that pastors are placed on a pedestal. Their argument is that pastors are human and as humans should be expected to be neither more nor less a sinner than others. Yes, we are all human and all sinners. Nevertheless, we have a calling to be examples of a Christ-like life.

"As I begin ministry I hope to remember the need for integrity. The pastor that my father and I encountered on the

dead-end road probably had once felt the fervor and desire to preach the Gospel and minister to God's people that I now feel. I hope and pray that when I've been in ministry for several decades, I can look back and know that my passion for Christ is as least as real and strong as it is now and that my integrity is intact."

Boundaries

Unfortunately, the story told by this student could be repeated many times with only a few altered details. As a pastoral counselor I have heard many sad stories about boundary violations in ministry. Most of these boundary violations started in helping relations, usually in counseling situations. I've counseled pastors and spouses after boundary sexual involvement with parishioners and served as a consultant to churches where sexual misconduct caused the dismissal of their spiritual leader. I've grieved over colleagues who lost their integrity and their right to continue in ministry, because they crossed the ethical and legal boundaries of a counseling relationship. For some time I struggled to understand how this could happen to well-trained, respected, and trusted people. I believe the problem is theological as much as it is legal and moral. The theological dynamic of temptation, fall, and damnation need to be seriously studied before anyone considers becoming a pastoral counselor. In this book, however, I want to write about a concern that I have never seen in the literature on sexual misconduct by theologically trained counselors and pastors. My primary purpose here is to write about the beginning of the problem, with the issue of confidentiality.

There is a long tradition in western societies of the right of clergy confidentiality. Civil laws protect the confessional as a privileged relationship. With the possible exception of imminent danger to someone's life or commission of a felony, pastors are not required to reveal information shared in confidence. This right and duty of pastors to keep conversations confidential is frequently tested by misinformed attorneys who do not realize that pastors have the same legal protection of privileged information as they do. Pastors have been willing to go to jail for refusing to reveal the content of confidential information in a court of law.

Codes of ethics of professional counseling organizations are very clear about the clergy's duty to maintain information shared in a counseling relationship in a confidential manner. Pastoral counselors have been expelled from these organizations for violating this code. Parish pastors have been forced to leave their churches because they betrayed the confidence of parishioners by carelessly sharing information from counseling or pastoral care conversations.

Confidentiality is a two-edged sword that can cut as easily one way as the other. On the one hand, the pastor has a legal right to privileged communication. On the other hand, the pastor can be punished for not keeping pastoral conversations confidential.

While confidentiality can be beneficial to a counseling relationship, it also can become a disguise for the destructive power of a professional landmine. I believe the secret to this paradox of blessing and curse is best found in the meaning of the word *confidentiality*. It comes from *confidere,* which means "to show confidence by imparting secrets." It also means "confidence, a relation of trust or intimacy." Confidence is considered a source of strength to protect counselees, and yet it has the potential power to destroy both counselees and counselors.

Epistolary Literature

While researching for this book, I came across "epistolary literature," a very popular genre of writing in the eighteenth century, a time that coincided with the early development of the postal systems in Europe and the new world of the colonies. This literature in letter format can help us understand the hidden dangers of confidentiality, especially since the genre is again gaining in popularity.

Janet Altman's *Epistolarity* helped me reflect upon the dynamics of temptation in a confidential relationship. She defines *epistolarity* as "the use of a letter's format properties to create meaning."[36] She claims that the confidant theme of novels was borrowed from classical theater in which the characters confided secrets to each other. In epistolarity literature the letter serves as a means for confiding secrets to a confidant who is to keep the secrets confidential.

Epistolary literature can be used to describe the action of counseling. The characters are the counselor and the counselee(s) in this improvised drama called counseling. They live in a narrative plot in a specific time frame. All the elements of tragedy and comedy, pathos and irony, are potentially present in the process of counseling. The setting is located where the dialogue proceeds without the visible presence of the audience. Community is excluded because counseling is essentially a private relationship that becomes an intimate relationship because it is by nature confidential.

In order to have confidentiality the counselee must have confidence in the confid*ant* (counselor) who protects the covenant of confidentiality. This is the only way the counselee will confide in the confid*ant*. The counselor (confid*ant*) listens to the stories, often in the form of confessions, of the confid*ent* (counselee). This is an active rather than a passive listening. With varying degrees of responses and questions, the confid*ant* encourages and influences revelations of the soul of the confid*ent*. The counselee (confid*ent*) takes on the role of the hero, not unlike in a play. The counselee (confid*ent*) in the act of storying experiences tells of old and new elements of the stories from the gist of stored memory. From narrating experiences with the language of thoughts, feelings and decisions new information emerges. The counselor's careful listening and responses to previously unknown or forgotten secrets of the protagonist and antagonist, of the counselee (confid*ent*) life stories helps create new or reauthored stories.

A trained counselor usually has a personality that is well delineated from the counselee. However; the counselor (confid*ant*) accumulates power in the helping relationship. This power can be beneficent or abusive in the confines of confidentiality. If you look closely at the pin or badge of a physician, you will see two snakes wound around a cross. One of the snakes represents the power to heal, the other the power to harm or kill. The symbolic power of the two snakes on the caduceus can be generated in the process of confiding. This makes counseling a powerful means for healing and also a potential means for doing great harm.

After several counseling sessions, the counselor (confid*ant*) and the counselee (confid*ent*) may find themselves in the middle of the minefield of intimacy created by the confidential relationship. Life (Eros) and death (Thanatos) surround them, but they are unaware of this powerful dynamic. The counselor (confid*ant*) has the responsibility of establishing and maintaining very clear professional boundaries. Otherwise the tempter uses the disguise of spirituality to destroy them. The spirituality of intimacy has such a powerfully explosive force that it is often unrecognized even by a theologically trained counselor.

Counselees look to pastors to help them find God by integrating their spirituality with other concerns in their lives. This is especially true of those who have been wounded by sexual abuse. The hunger for healing from the pain caused by the abuser also creates a longing for spiritual healing, for a more healthy intimacy. The vulnerable pastoral counselor (confid*ant*) can easily become a perpetuator of the evil, one who increases the wounds of abuse by a misguided attempt to heal with affection. Courage and strength are needed to love someone enough not to use them, but to become an instrument of God's *agape* love. A theologically trained counselor can easily be tricked into believing the spiritual and physical dimensions of intimacy can easily be merged into one, thus erasing the boundaries between right and wrong.

Pastors represent help because they represent God, the creator of divine and human love, but pastors have the same hungers for spiritual and sexual wholeness as do their counselees. Many are led into the ministry in search of healing from their own alienation from God and from self. When the intimacy of the counseling relationship replaces, or supplements intimacy with another human being, counseling can become an escape from God. Thus the double bind: "Physician heal thyself," while at the same time trying to help others find healing. The pastoral counselor who lacks an intimate personal relationship with God, as well as accountability to a community of faith for personal behavior, is walking blindly through the counseling minefield. Trafficking in the things of God through a pastoral role identity makes it easier to play God while attempting to save others through counseling. Ultimately, both souls are lost in the drama of a confidential relationship, thus creating a tragedy for both parties and the community of faith that bestowed the trust of confidentiality.

In this chapter I have described how confidentiality, that good and beneficial professional ethical practice, is the potentially explosive power that can destroy both the confid*ant* and the confid*ent*. Intimacy develops as confidences are shared by both the confid*ent* with the confid*ant*. The confessional creates a unique bonding between two individuals. Secret conversations tinged with fatality have the potential of seduction. Like the priest in George Sands' *Mademoiselle La Quintine*, the pastoral counselor is led to destruction when the role of priest-confessor is abandoned in favor of the status of friend-confidant.

The first stage of professional boundary violations begins when mutual confidences are shared between the counselor and the counselee. When the counselor-confid*ant* becomes the confid*ent*, the counselor now has a counselee who switches roles in the drama of counseling to become his confid*ant*. This reversal of roles sets the stage for the next exciting, but tragic episodes in the counseling relationship. The counselor now becomes the seducer under the protection of a confidential counseling relationship. The tempter has seduced the counselor into believing that it is sometimes necessary to confess one's own concerns to the counselee. Once the counselee becomes the personal confid*ant* of the counselor the first stage in boundary violations has been crossed.

The next steps lead directly to the landmine that destroys a healing counseling relationship. The paradox is that the practice of confidentiality, necessary to the integrity of the counseling relationship, can also become the potential cause of the destruction of both the counselor and the counselee. This possibility has often been overlooked in the training of pastors in seminaries and the continuing education seminars on pastoral ethics focused primarily upon an ethic of acts, rules, and the fear of legal consequences.

The mutual sharing of confidences between counselor and counselee, without accountability to the community, is destructive to the counselor, the counselee, and the community. The wounded healer is in danger of getting hopelessly lost in the minefield of counseling if he/she tries to do soul work (counseling) without accountability to someone outside of the counseling relationship. Confidentiality in counseling conversations is best maintained when the counselor has close personal relationships with family, friends, consultants and personal counselors to share personal concerns. Pastoral counselors need to be aware of the danger of sharing personal issues with counselees.

Mutual sharing is common among friends and support groups, but individual counseling is more than a friendship. It is a professional relationship in which one person seeks help from another, without anticipating the same kind of help in return.

The study of the psychological dynamics of sexual misconduct has produced some useful information for understanding sexual misconduct of pastors. What I'm suggesting here is that we also include the theological dynamics of the temptation/fall, biblical narrative. Damnation stories also include conversation that pretends to help someone. The Tempter is a good conversationalist. Discernment is needed to distinguish the difference between the Tempter and the Holy Spirit as guide of a counselor.

Character formation, built upon Christian virtue ethics, is needed to help pastoral counselors. "Damage control ethics" [37] that creates codes and ethic committees to protect pastors by publishing specific rules and guidelines for behavior may help pastors think twice before committing sexual misconduct; however, more is needed when faced with the temptation to use a counselee for one's own personal counseling.

Reverence for God and reverence for the personhood of the counselee is essential when we are tempted to use another person for our own satisfaction. Character is formed, or destroyed, by our management, or mismanagement, of pain and pleasure. In times when we are tempted to use another person for our own pleasure boundaries will depend upon the kind of character that has been developed by the disciplined habits of a virtuous life, also known as, "the fruit of the Spirit."

Confidentiality depends upon the character of the counselor. Certain rules apply, but the primary purpose of confidentiality is to guard the integrity of the counselee, thus creating the trust necessary to share the innermost secrets of the heart. The counselee is not bound, or necessarily committed, to maintain confidentiality.

Counseling is a one-way commitment to confidentiality.

Guarding the stories and confessions of a counselor is too much to be expected of a person sufficiently troubled enough to seek counseling; rather it should be seen for what it really is: an overt attempt of seduction. The counselor (confid*ant*) seeks to seduce the counselee (confid*ent*) by turning the counseling relationship into an opportunity to unburden his/her own soul. This seduction through confession of the counselor's struggles then puts pressure on the counselee to offer help to the counselor in a way that will help heal the emotional pain. This, in turn, creates further intimacy between the two confidantes. A land mine of passion builds until the trigger is pulled to release an explosion of physical intimacy. When this happens the Tempter again has used the privacy of confidentiality to destroy and kill. The wounded souls are temporarily healed by the fruit of temptation only to end up being cast out of the garden with deeper and longer lasting wounds.

Notes

1. John Dominic Crossan, *The Dark Interval: Towards a Theology of Story.* Niles, Illinois: Argus, 1975, p. 11.

2. Kevin M. Brandt, *Story as a Way of Knowing.* Kansas City, Missouri: Sheed & Ward, 1997, p. ix.

3. Kevin M. Brant, op. cit. p.11.

4. Kevin M. Brant. op. cit., p. 11

5. Jerome Bruner, *Actual Minds, Possible Worlds.* Cambridge, Massachusetts: Harvard University Press, 1986, p. 13.

6. Cheryl Mattingly and Linda C. Garro, "Narrative Representations of Ilnessess and Healing," *Social Science*, Vol. 38, No. 6, 1994, pp. 771-774.

7. Jerome Bruner, op. cit., 14.

8. Barbara Hardy, "Towards a Poetic of Fiction: An Approach Through Narrative," *Novel*, Vol. 2, No. 1, Fall 1968, p. 5.

9. Jerome Bruner, op. cit. p. 26.

10. Barry Lopez, *Crow and Weasel*, San Francisco: North Point Press, 1990, p. 60.

11. Carl R. Rogers, "Some Elements of Effective Interpersonal Communication," Speech given at California Institute of Technology, Pasadena, California, November 9, 1964, p. 4

12. Elochurkwu E. Uzukwu, *A Listening Church: Automony and Communion in African Churches.* Maryknoll, New York: Orbis Books, 1996, p.142.

13. Dietrich Bonhoeffer, *Life Together*, New York: Harper and Row, 1954, p. 97.

14. Jackson, Thomas, ed. *The Works of John Wesley*. "The Witness of Our Own Spirit," Schmael Publishers, Salem, Ohio, 1978. Vol. 5, Sermon 12, p. 138.

15. Lynn Hoffman, "Beyond Power and Control: Toward a Second-Order Family Systems Therapy." *Family Systems Medicine,* vol. 3. p.381-396.

16. Davies, Bronwyon Harre and Roym "The Discursive Production of Selves," *Journal for the Theory of Social Behavior,* Vol. 20, p. 1.

17. McNamee, Shelia and Gergen, Kenneth J, "The Client Is the Expert: A Not-Knowing Approach to Therapy," *Therapy as Social Construction,* ed. Harlene Anderson and Harold Goolishan. London: Sage Publications, 1992, p. 28.

18. McNamee, Bronwyon Harre and Roym. op. cit. p. 5.

19. Heije Faber and Ebel van der Schoot, *The Art of Pastoral Conversation.* Abingdon Press, Nashville, 1965, p. 8.

20. Heije Faber and Ebel van der Schoot, op. cit. p.25.

21. Douglas Purnell, *Conversation as Ministry.* Cleveland: The Pilgrim Press, 2003, p. 74.

22. Michael White and David Epston, *Narrative Means to Therapeutic Ends,* New York: W. W. Norton and Company, 1990, p. 40.

23. Hans Georg Gadamer, *Truth and Method,* Continuum, New York, 1994, p. 379.

24. Hans Georg Gadamer, op. cit., p. 375.

25. Monk, Winslade, Crocket, Kathie and Epston, *Narrative Therapy in Practice: The Archeology of Hope.* San Francisco: Jossey-Bass, 1977, p. 88.

26. Monk, Winslade, Crocket, Katie and Epston, op. cit. p. 264.

27. McNamee, Shelia and Gergen, Kenneth. *Therapy as Social Construction.* London: Sage Publications, 1992, p. 132-134.

28. Donald A. Schon, *The Reflective Practitioner.* New York: Basic Books, 1983, p. 161-162.

29. McNamee and Gergen, op. cit., 37.

30. Hans Georg Gadamer, op. cit., p. 365.

31. Michael Michaklo, "Thinking Like a Genius" *The Futurist,* September-October 2003, p. 51-56

32. Michael Michaklo, op. cit., p. 51.

33. Michael Michaklo, op. cit. p. 55.

34. Ricoeur, Paul. *Time and Narrative*. Chicago: The University of Chicago Press, 1984, vol. 1, p. 76.

35. Michael White and David Epston, op. cit., p. 125.

36. Altman, Janet. *Epistolarity: Approaches to Form*. Columbus, Ohio: Ohio State University Press, 1982, p. 4.

37. Gill, David W. *Becoming Good: Building Moral Character,* Inter Varsity Press, 2000, p.18.